Elizabeth Gaskell

Kate Flint

Northcote House

in association with
The British Council

WRITERS AND THEIR WORK

ISOBEL ARMSTRONG
General Editor

BRYAN LOUGHREY
Advisory Editor

© Copyright 1995 by Kate Flint

First published in 1995 by Northcote House Publishers Ltd, Plymbridge House,
Estover Road, Plymouth PL6 7PZ, United Kingdom.
Tel: (01752) 735251. Fax: (01752) 695699.

British Library Cataloguing-in-Publication Data
A catalogue record for this book is available from the British Library

ISBN 0 7463 0718 7

Typeset by PDQ Typesetting, Newcastle-Under-Lyme
Printed and bound in the United Kingdom by BPC Wheatons Ltd, Exeter

ELIZABETH GASKELL
from a chalk drawing by GEORGE RICHMOND *of 1851*
National Portrait Gallery

Contents

Acknowledgements

I offer warm thanks to Isobel Armstrong for her careful and perspicacious reading of the manuscript, and for her support throughout. I am particularly grateful to those students at the University of Oxford with whom I have discussed many of the ideas in this text. Any mistakes or infelicities are, of course, entirely my own.

Biographical Outline

1810 Elizabeth Cleghorn Stevenson born 29 September, to William Stevenson and Elizabeth (née) Holland.

1811 Death of mother; taken to live with her Aunt Hannah Lumb in Knutsford, Cheshire.

1828–9 Disappearance of her brother John at sea; went to live with father and stepmother in Chelsea, London.

1832 Married the Revd William Gaskell; moved to Manchester, where he was Assistant Minister at Cross Street Chapel.

1833 Stillbirth of daughter.

1834 Birth of daughter, Marianne.

1837 Poem, 'Sketches among the Poor', by Mr and Mrs Gaskell, appeared in *Blackwood's Magazine*. Birth of daughter, Margaret Emily (Meta).

c. 1838–41 Birth and death of a son.

1840 Description of Clopton Hall included in William Howitt's *Visits to Remarkable Places*.

1842 Birth of daughter, Florence Elizabeth.

1844 Birth of son, William.

1845 Death of son William.

1846 Birth of daughter, Julia Bradford.

1847 'Libbie Marsh's Three Eras', published in *Howitt's Journal*.

1848 *Mary Barton* published. 'Christmas Storms and Sunshine' appeared in *Howitt's Journal*.

1849 Met Dickens and other literary figures on visit to London. 'Hand and Heart' appeared in the *Sunday School Penny Magazine*; 'The Last Generation in England' in *Sartain's Union Magazine*, USA.

1850	*The Moorland Cottage* published. Dickens invited her to contribute to *Household Words*, in which appeared 'Lizzie Leigh', 'The Well of Pen Morfa' and 'The Heart of John Middleton'. First met Charlotte Brontë.
1851	First episode of *Cranford* appeared in *Household Words*. 'Mr Harrison's Confessions' published in *The Ladies' Companion*.
1852	'The Schah's English Gardener' and 'The Old Nurse's Story' appeared in *Household Words*, and 'Bessy's Trouble at Home' in the *Sunday School Penny Magazine*.
1853	*Ruth* and *Cranford* published. 'Cumberland Sheep-Shearers', 'Traits and Stories of the Huguenots', 'Morton Hall', 'My French Master' and 'The Squire's Story' appeared in *Household Words*.
1854	*North and South* began serialization in *Household Words*, where 'Modern Greek Songs' and 'Company Manners' were also published. William Gaskell became Minister of Cross Street Chapel.
1855	*North and South* and *Lizzie Leigh and Other Stories* published. 'An Accursed Race' and 'Half a Lifetime Ago' appeared in *Household Words*. The Revd Patrick Brontë asked her to write Charlotte's *Life*.
1856	'The Poor Clare' appeared in *Household Words*.
1857	*The Life of Charlotte Brontë* published.
1858	'My Lady Ludlow', 'Right at Last', and 'The Manchester Marriage' appeared in *Household Words*, and 'The Doom of the Griffiths' in *Harper's Magazine*.
1859	*Round the Sofa and Other Tales* published. 'Lois the Witch' and 'The Crooked Branch' appeared in Dickens's new magazine, *All the Year Round*.
1860	*Right at Last and other Tales* published. 'Curious, if True' appeared in *Cornhill Magazine*.
1861	'The Grey Woman' appeared in *All the Year Round*.
1863	*Sylvia's Lovers* published. 'A Dark Night's Work', 'An Italian Institution', 'The Cage at Cranford', and 'Crowley Castle' appeared in *All the Year Round*, and 'Cousin Phillis' in the *Cornhill Magazine*.
1864	'French Life' published in *Fraser's Magazine*, and *Wives and Daughters* began to appear in the *Cornhill*.
1865	*Cousin Phillis and Other Tales* and *The Grey Woman and*

Other Tales published. Bought house near Holybourne, Hampshire; died there, suddenly, on 12 November.

1866   *Wives and Daughters* published posthumously.

Abbreviations and References

MB	*Mary Barton*
C	*Cranford*
R	*Ruth*
NS	*North and South*
SL	*Sylvia's Lovers*
CP	*Cousin Phillis and Other Tales*
WD	*Wives and Daughters*
DNW	*A Dark Night's Work and Other Stories*

In all the above cases, the edition cited is that published by Oxford University Press in their World's Classics series.

CB	*The Life of Charlotte Brontë* (Everyman's Library)
CPT	*Cousin Phillis and Other Tales* (Everyman's Library)
L	*The Letters of Mrs Gaskell*, edited by J. A. V. Chapple and Arthur Pollard

1

The Life of
Elizabeth Gaskell

Elizabeth Gaskell (1810–65) wrote to her friend Eliza Fox about the difficulties she experienced in juggling the priorities in her life. She claims that she has 'a great number of "Mes"':

> and that's the plague. One of my mes is, I do believe a true Christian – (only people call her socialist and communist), another of my mes is a wife and mother, and highly delighted at the delight of everyone else in the house ... Now that's my 'social' self I suppose. Then again I've another self with a full taste for beauty and convenience whh is pleased on its own account. How am I to reconcile all these warring members? (L 108)

Gaskell was writing in 1850, after the appearance of *Mary Barton* (1848) and a couple of pieces of short fiction, but before the remainder of her major works appeared: *Ruth* (1853), *Cranford* (1853), *North and South* (1855), a biography, *The Life of Charlotte Brontë* (1857), *Sylvia's Lovers* (1863) and, posthumously, *Wives and Daughters* (1866). Additionally, she was to publish a number of shorter works. Some of these are novella length (*The Moorland Cottage*, 1850; *My Lady Ludlow*, 1858; *Cousin Phillis*, 1863); some are short stories; some, like 'The Last Generation in England' (1849), are part essay, part memoir. The diversity of these works appears in their subject matter, their form, and their relation to other genres: they are as evasive of easy generalization as Gaskell found her sense of herself to be.

The lines which Gaskell wrote to Eliza Fox are symptomatic of issues which recur throughout her writings. The theme of conflicting senses of identity is prominent in her fiction. So, too, is her manipulation of the tension which arises when individuals are subjected to rival demands, whether these demands come

1

from the claims others make on them, or from inner debates produced by moral dilemmas. In particular, Gaskell was aware of the various types of constraints faced both by women in general, during a period strongly affected by notions of social duties and propriety, and by the more specific pressures faced by a woman writer, especially one, like herself, with a family. As she wrote in *The Life of Charlotte Brontë*:

> When a man becomes an author, it is probably merely a change of employment to him. He takes a portion of that time which has hitherto been devoted to some other study or pursuit; he gives up something of the legal or medical profession, in which he has hitherto endeavoured to serve others, or relinquishes part of the trade or business by which he has been striving to gain a livelihood; and another merchant or lawyer, or doctor, steps into his vacant place, and probably does as well as he. But no other can take up the quiet, regular duties of the daughter, the wife, or the mother, as well as she whom God has appointed to fill that particular place: a woman's principal work in life is hardly left to her own choice; nor can she drop the domestic charges devolving on her as an individual, for the exercise of the most splendid talents that were ever bestowed. And yet she must not shrink from the extra responsibility implied by the very fact of her possessing such talents. She must not hide her gift in a napkin; it was meant for the use and service of others. In a humble and faithful spirit must she labour to do what is not impossible, or God would not have sent her to do it. (*CB* 238)

These sentences reaffirm Gaskell's concern with responsibility – and her recognition that accepting responsibility may not be easy.

Elizabeth Cleghorn Stevenson was born in 1810 to Unitarian parents, and the Unitarian faith was important to her throughout her life. It emphasized freedom of thought and the importance of rationality (although this did not impede a lifelong interest on Gaskell's part in superstition, dreams, and the supernatural). It stressed the existence of an underlying principle of social progress. This could be aided by scientific discovery, but above all was dependent upon the actions performed by the morally self-aware and responsible individual. Posing a challenge to this meliorist view of history were, of course, the problems evidenced by the existence of social hardship, and by the daily defeats and tragedies suffered by individuals in their everyday lives. Thus

Gaskell's fiction is marked by a tension created through the opposition of optimism and pain. In turn, her writing both demands from the reader a rational response, as the workings of industrial society or of family dynamics are laid bare in front of us with a good deal of convincing circumstantial detail, and deliberately plays on the reader's emotions, often employing conspicuously fictional devices of melodrama and coincidence to this end.

Gaskell's mother died when she was barely a year old: the young girl went to live with relatives in Knutsford, Cheshire, experiencing a genteel, self-protective mode of life which was later to provide the inspiration and material for *Cranford*. The importance of the mother – and the irrevocability of her loss – is a corner-stone of the emotional foundations of Gaskell's fiction. In *Sylvia's Lovers*, for example, the narrator notes how Sylvia's mother used to wait for her at the close of day on a little grass knoll at the side of their farmhouse:

> and many a time in her after life, when no one cared much for her out-goings and in-comings, the straight, upright figure of her mother, fronting the setting sun, but searching through its blinding rays for a sight of her child, rose up like a sudden-seen picture, the remembrance of which smote Sylvia to the heart with a sense of a lost blessing, not duly valued while possessed. (*SL* 61)

The valuing of maternity is a theme which crops up even in brief, passing anecdotes. In *Cranford*, the wife of a travelling conjuror tells how she could not bear to lose her seventh child, like the previous six, to the Indian climate, and walked across country to make her passage home: 'the natives were very kind. We could not understand one another; but they saw my baby on my breast, and they came out to me, and brought me rice and milk, and sometimes flowers' (*C* 109). Most notably of all, the theme of the redeeming power of motherhood is central to the didactic message of *Ruth*.

Gaskell's father remarried: Gaskell visited her new family in London on occasion, but with little enjoyment. She was close to her brother John, twelve years older than herself, but rarely saw him. He went to sea in 1821, and never returned from a voyage to India in 1828. Again, the theme of loss and return proves central to Gaskell's fiction. Sometimes she wishfully uses the motif of someone being presumed drowned (Peter in *Cranford*; Charley Kinraid in *Sylvia's Lovers*) only to turn up again; sometimes, return from sea is fraught with danger, as in the case of Frederick Hale, in *North and South*, slipping into the country to see his dying mother, whilst under threat of death on suspicion of having caused a shipboard mutiny.

In 1832, Elizabeth married the Unitarian minister, William Gaskell, and moved from the provincial town of Knutsford to the rapidly expanding city of Manchester. Here, she became mother to four daughters, and to two sons who died in infancy. In *North and South*, Gaskell uses the device of the young and impressionable Margaret Hale arriving in Milton from the south of England as a means of showing how forcibly the city's appearance strikes an outsider. Margaret notes the taste and smell of smoke in the air; the pollution, which at first she takes to be a raincloud; the 'long, straight, hopeless streets of regularly-built houses' (*NS* 59); the people who jostle up against her in the streets, threatening her personal space, and who are forward enough to comment openly on her appearance. Her father, meanwhile, is struck – as Margaret later learns to be – by the power both of machinery and of the men. Gaskell's own initial reactions to Manchester may well have been very like Margaret's. It was a town of contrasts: of extremely poor housing and sanitation (as recorded by Friedrich Engels in *The Condition of the Working Class in England*, which appeared in Germany in 1845, as well as by such local English commentators as James Kay, *The Moral and Physical Conditions of the Working Classes Employed in the Cotton Manufacture of Manchester* (1832), and Joseph Adshead, *Distress in Manchester* (1842)). Trade depressions in the early 1840s, and again in 1846, increased the hardships experienced by working people and their families, and brought with them riots and threats of unrest.

Gaskell had direct knowledge of these hardships through helping her husband with his duties as Minister in charge of the Cross Street Chapel, distributing soup tickets, food and clothing through her work for the District Provident Society, a local philanthropic organization, and visiting the homes of her Sunday-school pupils. She saw at first hand the number of children who died from epidemics, the families who had to sell their furniture to buy food. Manchester became a centre for Chartist activity, when the workers, frustrated by their political powerlessness, sought redress through attempting to redefine the terms of parliamentary representation. Gaskell's own early fiction, in particular, can be linked to this desire for public representation, since it sets out to give a voice to the otherwise silent, whether the mill-worker or the unmarried working-class mother. Both *Mary Barton* and *Ruth* were not just topical, but interventionist in their attempt to arouse understanding and sympathy.

Yet at the same time, Manchester not only maintained a reputation for commercial and industrial energy, but was a growing centre of scientific and literary activity. The Gaskell family were directly involved in several cultural circles. A number of local businessmen and MPs worshipped at the Cross Street Chapel: their sense of their own rectitude and propriety was to be overtly challenged by the accusations they felt levelled against their number in *Mary Barton*, with its exposure of an apparent chasm of understanding between masters and men. Their values were challenged, too, by Gaskell's sympathetic treatment of an unmarried mother in *Ruth*. William Gaskell became professor of history, literature, and logic at Manchester New College from 1846 to 1853, and his strong interest in dialect and in the importance of localized linguistic forms reverberates throughout his wife's fiction. She appended his 'Two Lectures on Lancashire Dialect' to the 1854 edition of *Mary Barton*, for example, and took great care to differentiate Yorkshire from Lancashire dialect forms in *Sylvia's Lovers*.

Although the later 1840s and the 1850s saw a number of improvements in social conditions, the American Civil War led to a further collapse in the cotton trade in 1862–3, bringing with it renewed hardship. By the early 1860s, Gaskell's own life had changed considerably: as a well-established, well-regarded author, and with her daughters grown up, or nearly so, she led a professional life which took her away from Manchester for stretches at a time, to stay in London or travel on the Continent. Moreover, she was increasingly subject to – or increasingly subjected herself to – a demanding writing schedule. Nevertheless, despite the many professional pressures on her time, Gaskell was as active during the latter period of economic depression as she had been in the early 1840s, setting up sewing-schools to provide part-time work; corresponding with Florence Nightingale, whom she knew and admired, to see if some of the laid-off mill women might train as nurses. As her contact with Nightingale demonstrates, by this time, Gaskell's scope of acquaintances had widened considerably. Initially discreet about sharing her writing with others – to the extent of pretending to look for something she might have dropped under the table when breakfast discussion turned to the possible authorship of the anonymously published *Mary Barton* – Gaskell developed strong friendships with a range of literary personalities, including the poet and editor Mary Howitt, Harriet Martineau, and Anna Jameson. Although she and George Eliot never met, they exchanged some warm letters. They shared literary tastes, such as Wordsworth and Ruskin, and the concept of sympathy was crucial to the novels of both women. This was something reflected in private communication when Eliot thanked Gaskell for her praise of *Adam Bede*, calling hers 'one of the minds which is capable of judging as well as being moved ... I shall always love to think that one woman wrote to another such sweet encouraging words'.

Gaskell's connections with other women writers may be read in relation to the importance women's friendships hold throughout her fiction (although she was quick to recognize the power of rivalry and jealousy as well). These friendships often cross classes, as we see in the support which Dixon offers her employer, Mrs Hale, in *North and South* when she comforts Mrs Hale over her distress at moving away from the rural South, and then nurses her when she falls fatally ill. The bond of understanding between the two women is so close that Mrs Hale's daughter Margaret feels in danger of being supplanted. Loyalty and emotional sustenance are found, too, in the help which the servant Amante gives her mistress in 'The Grey Woman' (1861), enabling her to escape from her Bluebeard-like husband.

In such instances, as well as in Gaskell's more obviously staged scenes of class juxtaposition, emotional needs are seen as breaking down class boundaries: a dramatized recognition of the fact that we are all 'living, breathing, warm human creature[s]' (*SL* 301). Such a recognition, Gaskell suggests, may be more readily achievable in a domestic environment than in the more public world of the obviously hierarchized workplace. Nonetheless, it is the spirit which, ideally, she would care to see animating industrial relations as well. Thus she presents the manufacturer, Thornton, in *North and South*, coming into personal contact with the outspoken workman, Higgins: 'Once brought face to face, man to man, with an individual of the masses around him, and (take notice) *out* of the character of master and workman, in the first instance, they had each begun to recognise that "we have all of us one human heart" ' (*NS* 419). This intercourse which 'might not have the effect of preventing all future clash of opinion and action, when the occasion arose, would, at any rate, enable both master and man to look upon each other with far more charity and sympathy, and bear with each other more patiently and kindly' (*NS* 420). Gaskell's communicative model for successful human relations involves dialogue; the sharing of perspectives. To this end, her own fictional prose is marked, like her letters, with relaxed, conversational intimacy.

The most notable literary friendship which Gaskell formed was with Charlotte Brontë: notable partly, of course, since it led to her writing her biography after the younger novelist's early death – probably from complications connected with pregnancy – in 1855. The social conventionality of this biography has been picked up on by several commentators, since in part it represents a defence (not just of Charlotte, but of her sisters) against charges of wildness and impropriety. This involved the deliberate omission of Brontë's passionate attachment to Monsieur Héger (the prototype for Paul Emanuel in *Villette*); more generally it caused Gaskell to comment on the special, isolated circumstances in which the Brontë sisters had grown up. Thus she draws attention to the fact that they received little womanly influence in their childhoods: 'owing to Mrs. Brontë's death so soon after her husband had removed into the district, and also to the distances, and the bleak country to be traversed, the wives of [Mr Brontë's] clerical friends did not accompany their husbands [on their visits to Haworth]; and the daughters grew up out of childhood into girlhood bereft, in a singular manner, of all such society as would have been natural to their age, sex, and station' (*CB* 33).

Moreover, Gaskell tends to emphasize Charlotte's domesticity, her womanliness, so that, notwithstanding Charlotte's own reservations on the subject, marriage to Arthur Nicholls is presented as though it provided the romantic apotheosis towards which her life had been tending. Domestic felicity is put forward as something to be relished, with no hint that it might compromise the exercise of her subject's particular literary talents. Thus Gaskell quotes from the letters sent her by Charlotte Brontë after her marriage as illustrative of 'the low murmurs of happiness we, who listened, heard' (CB 396). The tenor of the letters she quotes suggests, though, an almost perverse deafness on Gaskell's part. Brontë writes: 'My own life is more occupied than it used to be: I have not so much time for thinking: I am obliged to be more practical... [Arthur] often finds a little work for his wife to do, and I hope she is not sorry to help him. I believe it is not bad for me that his bent should be so wholly towards matters of life and active usefulness; so little inclined to the literary and contemplative' (CB 397).

Yet, despite recognizing Gaskell's biases, it would be over-simplistic to pigeon-hole this biography as conservative. In the stress which falls on everyday domestic detail lies one of the elements which allow us to claim this biography as in some ways experimental. The centre of interest falls not on a notable person's existence in a public arena, but lies in the privileged access to personal thoughts which we are shown through letters, and through conversations reconstructed from notes. We are deliberately shown Charlotte Brontë the private woman, as well as the writing figure. To do so was to revise mid-nineteenth-century expectations about what it was suitable to include in a biography. It is, moreover, a biography in which the particular emphases chosen by Gaskell function on occasion as autobiographical comment. As though tacitly reflecting on the confusion of identities she herself felt, Gaskell presents Brontë as being able to draw clear lines of demarcation between these two spheres. After the publication of *Jane Eyre* in 1846, Gaskell wrote:

> Henceforward Charlotte Brontë's existence becomes divided into two parallel currents – her life as Currer Bell, the author; her life as Charlotte Brontë, the woman. There were separate duties belonging to each character – not opposing each other, not impossible, but difficult to be reconciled. (CB 237–8)

That a woman, particularly a married woman with a family, like herself, could find such reconciliation just about impossible, was – as we have seen – all too apparent to Elizabeth Gaskell. Simultaneously, though, she did regard such a dual career as one which could bring advantages with it. Corresponding with an aspiring woman writer, she noted that experiencing 'the interests of a wife and mother' will enable one to bring understanding and compassion – both very necessary virtues – to one's novels: 'a good writer of fiction must have *lived* an active & sympathetic life if she wishes her books to have strength & vitality in them' (*L* 695). Indeed, she suggested in a letter to another friend, the painter Eliza Fox, that writing, art or music could provide an extremely necessary escape: 'I am sure it is healthy for [women] to have the refuge of the hidden world of Art to shelter themselves in when too much pressed upon by daily small Lilliputian arrows of peddling cares' (*L* 106).

Yet as someone who always poured her energies into whatever she was involved with – whether writing fiction or correspondence, socializing or sorting out family problems – Elizabeth Gaskell was never successfully able to compartmentalize her own life. The strain took its toll on her heart. Although she did not die as young as Charlotte Brontë, she was only 55 at the time of her death, of sudden heart failure, in 1864. She left *Wives and Daughters*, which was being serialized in the *Cornhill Magazine*, nearly, but not quite, finished. Set back in the time of her childhood, this is a novel which encapsulates many of the themes which she explored and developed throughout her writing career: the relationship between parents and children; domestic difficulties set against wider patterns of social change; tensions posed by divided loyalties, and by short versus long-term expeditiousness in matters of truthfulness. Yet despite being located in the past, this is nonetheless, a post-Darwinian novel, with one of the most prominent male figures, Roger Hamley, being drawn directly from Darwin himself.

Darwin's own conclusions, with their emphasis on the interconnectedness of the natural world, and on the jostling for survival which takes place within it, owe much in their formulation to the intellectual atmosphere out of which Gaskell's own writing emerged. The presence of Hamley, and the fact of his 'scientific voyage, with a view to bringing back specimens of the fauna of distant lands' (*WD* 378), in the provincial world of *Wives and Daughters* serves as a paradigm, in many ways, for Gaskell's own work. Whilst her settings are ones that she herself knew well, or researched meticulously, and whilst the bulk of her plots revolve around domestic dramas, wider social and intellectual issues continually intersect with her interest in individual human lives.

Recent criticism of Elizabeth Gaskell has concentrated on two separate aspects of her work: her writing as a 'social problem' novelist, and hence her role in supporting or challenging the dominant ideological positions of her time; and the fact of her being a woman writer. This short study sets out to show that, for Gaskell, these two facets of her writing were inextricably linked: as indivisible as those 'warring members' which, she felt, made up her own composite sense of identity. Connecting these two facets is a concern with the problem of authority, something which provides a continuous, if tacit, thread throughout her novels. Who is most capable of wielding authority within society, and how might it best be exercised? What is the relationship between secular and religious authority? On what claims may authority be based? On experience, on first-hand knowledge, or the strength of moral beliefs? Gaskell interrogates the relationship between class and authority, hence partially revealing, and to some extent calling into question, the means by which power circulates within society.

Inseparable from the representation of authority is the position of the author herself. Particularly in Elizabeth Gaskell's earlier fiction, the narrative voice manifests unease and uncertainty about its role. One cannot prove whether such uncertainty mirrors Gaskell's personal unease, or is a strategy employed to develop a relationship of equality and intimacy with the reader. What may confidently be stated is that Gaskell never seizes the opportunity to adopt a fully authoritative stance towards her readers. Although she may guide in certain interpretive directions, she leaves it up to her readers to draw judgements, assessments, conclusions from the events she puts before them. The ultimate authority, in Gaskell's work, is that which readers are invited to develop for themselves.

2

Mary Barton

Elizabeth Gaskell's first novel, *Mary Barton* (1848), took its direct impetus from both public and private concerns. On the one hand, Gaskell was moved, as she states in the novel's preface, by her 'deep sympathy with the care-worn men' (*MB* xxxv) whom she saw daily in the streets of Manchester, and by her commiseration with their sense of bitter injustice that their plight seemed to be ignored by the prosperous, especially by 'the masters whose fortunes they had helped to build up' (*MB* xxxv). She wished to 'give some utterance to the agony which, from time to time, convulses this dumb people' (*MB* xxxvi), and to cause her readers to reflect 'on this unhappy state of things between those so bound to each other by common interests, as the employers and the employed must ever be' (*MB* xxxv–xxxvi).

At the same time, Gaskell was seeking an outlet for her own personal agony: the trauma of losing her son, William, from scarlet fever when he was only nine months old. When she remarks, in *Mary Barton*: 'Oh! I do think that the necessity for exertion, for some kind of action (bodily or mentally) in time of distress, is the most infinite blessing' (*MB* 288), she is drawing a general principle from her own immediate experience. Significantly, it is through acknowledging that pain – the pain felt at the loss of a child – can cross class boundaries, that the gap between employer and employee (and, for that matter, between reader and working-class character) is temporarily dissolved within this novel.

Mary Barton has customarily been called a social problem novel, and classified alongside, for example, Benjamin Disraeli's *Sybil* (1845) and Charles Kingsley's *Alton Locke* (1850). The genre had, however, already established itself as particularly popular among women writers, thanks to works by, for example, Harriet

11

Martineau, Frances Trollope, Charlotte Elizabeth Tonna and Eliza Meteyard. Arguably, because of its charitable, caring implications, it provided an opportunity for women to be able to write about public issues without being openly chided for being 'unfeminine'. It was certainly a means whereby those with no political representation could hope to influence political decisions. Gaskell's novel deals not with the workplace, but with the effects of urban employment – and, more especially, unemployment – upon the family. The early chapters of the novel focus on the Bartons, exploring the reactions of John Barton (the novel was originally to have borne his name as its title) to the increasing poverty he sees around him at a time when the depression in trade meant lower wages, shorter hours, and fewer mill workers employed. By contrast:

> Carriages still roll along the streets, concerts are still crowded by subscribers, the shops for expensive luxuries still find daily customers, while the workman loiters away his unemployed time in watching these things, and thinking of the pale, uncomplaining wife at home, and the wailing children asking in vain for enough of food, – of the sinking health, of the dying life of those near and dear to him. The contrast is too great. Why should he alone suffer from bad times? (*MB* 24)

Through a series of scenes, such as her contrast of the Davenports' fetid cellar with the luxuriant atmosphere of the mill-owner Carson's home, Gaskell establishes the context in which a desperate working man might first turn to Chartism, and then let his name go forward in the ballot to determine who should assassinate Carson's son.

The dramatic impact of this murder is intensified, in fictional terms, by the fact that Harry Carson had been pursuing Barton's daughter, Mary. Although it is Barton who drew the fatal lot and committed the murder, suspicion naturally falls on Mary's other suitor, the rising workman and engineer, Jem Wilson. Mary, who suddenly wakes up to the knowledge, even before Harry's death, that she vastly preferred Jem of the two, knows him to be innocent. Obeying Gaskell's premise about the advisability of acting decisively, she successfully chases to Liverpool to bring back the crucial witness who can provide Jem's alibi. In open court, moreover, Mary puts aside 'womanly' modesty to speak of her love for Jem over Harry Carson. Her father, meanwhile, cannot escape the punishment of his own conscience. He confesses the murder to Mr Carson, and asks his forgiveness. Despite the fact that he does not initially receive this forgiveness, Barton himself can acknowledge that he is observing not the obduracy of an oppressive master, but the pain of someone who, like himself many years before, had lost a son: 'Rich and poor, masters and men, were then brothers in the deep suffering of the heart' (*MB* 431). Yet Carson witnesses, by chance, an instance of forgiveness taking place in the street; and, returning home to read his Bible, is led to reconsider his responses. He goes back to Barton's house, and the workman dies in his arms. Providence, and the power of biblical narrative – not to mention Gaskell's manipulation of the fictional techniques of parallelism and coincidence – have accomplished what political interventions cannot.

Mary and Jem emigrate to a new life in Canada. To some extent, this emigration is forced on Jem by the demands of probability. He knows from previous experience (and simultaneously Gaskell shows her understanding of the practical dynamics of the workplace) that factory workers are often unwilling to work alongside those over whom hangs some suspicion of crime: he is therefore not surprised when it is intimated to him that he would do well not to work in Manchester for a while. Moreover, emigration was one possible solution for an ambitious young man at a time of trade depression. But the ending may also be read as evasive, even pessimistic, in the sense that the problems of industrial England, despite the 'improvements' which we hear of Carson as making, are not finally tackled head-on. It is the Canadian scene which carries the emotional weight at the end of the novel, whilst such optimism as is expressed about improvements in Manchester's industrial relations is left in abstract terms of Christian virtues and unspecified remedies.

Yet it is important that we do not think of *Mary Barton* as a novel which might be expected to offer solutions to the problems which it depicts. This is apparent from the cavalier way in which Gaskell treats Chartism. Whereas the main points of the Chartists (universal male suffrage, equal electoral districts, annual parliaments, a secret ballot, and the abolition of property qualifications for Members of Parliament) would, if accepted, have meant real changes in the composition of Parliament, and the right of working men to Parliamentary representation, Gaskell never

13

spells them out in this novel. Instead, she characterizes Chartists as 'wild and visionary', although acknowledging that being visionary at least 'shows a soul, a being not altogether sensual; a creature who looks forward for others, if not for himself' (*MB* 199). The most direct potential political route to change is hence heavily muffled.

Rather, the novel aims at awakening a spirit of compassion and sympathy in the reader, at getting him or her to 'look forward for others'. Recognizing this helps one to understand some of its apparent inconsistencies, particularly its shifts in points of view. The narrator qualifies the passage quoted above, in which John Barton speaks out against his sense of social injustice, in terms which suddenly pander to middle-class sensibilities: 'I know that this is not really the case; and I know what is the truth in such matters: but what I wish to impress is what the workman feels and thinks' (*MB* 24). At one level, Gaskell here takes refuge within a dominant class position, lest she alienate her reader. But we are also being asked to accept the relativity of truths: Barton's perception that those who hurry in and out of the 'well-filled, well-lighted shops' (*MB* 70) on the London Road are all joyful is accurate enough so far as he is concerned. Moreover, Gaskell turns round his reductive capacity for generalization from external impressions, so that it acts as a warning to the reader not to judge from superficial appearances alone, rather as Thomas Carlyle's *Sartor Resartus* (1838) is an extended admonition against judging a man by his clothes. Thus the distinction between protagonist, author, and reader at the level of perception is obliterated: they all have inevitably partial angles on reality:

> he could not, you cannot, read the lot of those who daily pass you by in the street. How do you know the wild romances of their lives; the trials, the temptations they are even now enduring, resisting, sinking under? (*MB* 70)

Nor should the strong, melodramatic narrative line be judged against criteria of realistic probability, despite the circumstantial accuracy of the novel's settings (assassinations, for example, were rare if not unknown at the time, but, as Gaskell put it, she wished to show 'to what lengths the animosity of irritated workmen would go' (*L* 196). More profitably, it may be seen as a technique of seizing the readers' interest, and encouraging their active emotional involvement in the plot. What is more, as we have just seen, Gaskell readily employs a literary register – 'the wild romances of their lives' – in an attempt to convey the intensity of feeling experienced by those whose lives an ignorant reader might be tempted to dismiss as prosaic.

At first reading, the plot of *Mary Barton* may seem to shift in its focus during its course. During the first half, the novel is concerned with documenting social and political issues, presenting us not just with shocking extremes of poverty, but with the perilous nature of working-class prosperity, as Gaskell shows the gradual disappearance of minutely detailed items of furniture – like the japanned tea-tray – from the Barton home as their resources dwindled. The reader's understanding of the recent roots of working-class life is encouraged through a demonstration of the tenuous, but still present links with a rural past, through the elderly Alice Wilson's nostalgia for her country childhood, and through Job Leigh's interests as a naturalist. Social inequality is brought out not just by means of set-piece scenes, but in the way casual assumptions are shown to be made. A policeman witnesses the discussion between Harry Carson and Jem Wilson about the former's intentions concerning Mary. Harry loses his temper with Jem, and strikes him across the face with his cane. The workman understandably retaliates, and knocks him flying. The policeman comes forward, pinions Jem, and inquires of Harry whether he should 'take him to the lock-ups for assault, sir?' (*MB* 211). The social assumptions made by the policeman, the figure of authority in this scene and, apparently, the representative of the mill-owners' class interests, are left to speak for themselves.

In making the heroine of her novel a working woman, Gaskell enabled the introduction into her fiction of various particularly topical issues: issues often passed over by the earlier commentators on 'social problem' fiction with their limited conceptions of 'social problems' as things which might ultimately be sorted out through legislation, or by a reordering of class relations. First, the very issue of women working at all is raised in a conversation between Mary and Mrs Wilson, the latter claiming that she knows nine men who have been driven to the public house because their wives work in factories, and who thus are deprived of a bright home and fire to return to: 'it's Prince Albert as ought to be asked how he'd like his missis to be from home when he comes in, tired

15

and worn, and wanting some one to cheer him' (*MB* 140). This is a strong protest which Gaskell makes no direct attempt to counterbalance: she seems to use the occasion as a means of consolidating the desirability of bourgeois domestic ideology, something which, once again, may be seen as a means of aligning herself with the values of many of her readers in a manœuvre designed simultaneously to gain their trust and prove her own respectability.

She raises further contentious issues during the first half of the novel through the fact of Mary working for a milliner and dressmaker, a notorious occupation for a young Victorian woman; one which, embodying counterbalancing imagery of domestic duty – the act of sewing – with the moral danger which its public practice brought with it, had a particular fascination for 'social problem' novelists such as Francis Paget, with *The Pageant* (1843), and Elizabeth Stone, in *The Young Milliner* (1843), and artists like Robert Redgrave (*The Sempstress*, 1846) and Anna Blunden, whose painting *For only one short hour* ... (1854) took its title from Thomas Hood's widely known poem of protest, *The Song of the Shirt*:

> For only one short hour
> To feel as I used to feel,
> Before I knew the woes of want
> And the walk that costs a meal.

As Gaskell amplifies in *Ruth*, not only were the hours long and demanding, and hence damaging to health, there was a tendency for employers in this field to choose only pretty girls, who would adorn the work-room; who would appear, at times, in public with the dressmakers' creations, and enhance the image of feminine beauty on which business depended. The temptation for women workers to fall to the blandishments of young men who were attracted to such an apparently ready and approachable source of attractive, commodified female forms emerging onto the street late at night seems – at least in the public eye – to have been strong: strong enough for the contemporary reader to feel a quiver of apprehension when we learn that the young Harry Carson, 'unfettered by work-hours, let scarcely a day pass without contriving a meeting with the beautiful little milliner [Mary, in other words] he had first seen while lounging in a shop where his sisters were making some purchases' (*MB* 91). Gaskell understands a part of his attraction for the 'ambitious' Mary: he was rich, and a gentleman, although the reader is instantly warned against any sympathetic feeling towards him through the condescension of 'beautiful little milliner' and the casual dilettantism conveyed through 'lounging'. But Mary's aunt, Esther, is introduced as a dreadful warning of the dangers of loving across class barriers, reminding one of the potential future in store for the woman, who will inevitably be betrayed. However, it is important to acknowledge that Esther is presented as more than an apocalyptic warning as to what can happen to a woman who 'falls'. It is she who brings the crucial evidence concerning the identity of Harry Carson's murderer, which spurs Mary into the action which will eventually clear Jem's name. And although she dies of consumption, which might seem like a form of punishment for her career as a prostitute, this is not before Mary has, significantly, confused her form and voice with that of her dead mother. Mother and magdalene, two apparently opposi-tional linchpins of Victorian iconography, are thus controversially collapsed into one, suggesting that the possibility of redemptive force may, through one's innate maternal capacities, lie with all categories of women. Such a generalization, binding women through biology, is to be called into question, however, in Gaskell's later works of fiction.

Gaskell's capacity for seizing on individualizing details in her descriptions, as well as the relative fidelity with which she records dialect forms and speech patterns, underpins this novel with an authority drawn from direct observation. In the second half, however, although Gaskell does not jettison her eye for detail or ear for local language, the story line is increasingly occupied by Mary's quest to redeem Jem. Social comment seems to give way to the demands of a romance plot. The exception would seem to be the chapter near the end where Job Leigh meets with Mr Carson, and the desire 'that a perfect understanding, and complete confidence and love, might exist between masters and men' (*MB* 457), is once again spelt out: however, this chapter was not part of Gaskell's original plan, but was added when John Chapman, her publisher, found that he was short of material to make up the third number of the novel.

But the two halves of the plot are inextricably linked by the issues of power and powerlessness: economic and sexual exploitation are shown as going hand in hand. In presenting the organized efforts of the working men, as exemplified by the Chartists' petition, as ultimately ineffectual, yet showing how Mary's determined action results in justice being done in one specific case, Gaskell offers the reader the concept of an alternative source of power from that which is caught up in the industrialized forms of patriarchal relations between masters and men. She presents a democratic and domestic source of power which derives from inner qualities rather than from class position.

At times Mary is, of course, improbably idealized. Gaskell presents her with beauty untarnished by environment, and with a far less pronounced regional accent than that of most of her companions. She comforts Mrs Wilson, Jem's mother, with 'the influence of those sweet, loving blue eyes, those tears of sympathy, those words of love and hope' (*MB* 296): standard marks of womanly compassion. She is innately modest: we learn that she has 'whisperings of her womanly nature that caused her to shrink from any unmaidenly action' (*MB* 204). But for Gaskell, conventionality was not incompatible with strong action in a heroine. Even before the crucial crisis of the novel, we learn of Mary's strengths. Practical, she was not only used to managing the family finances out of necessity, but enjoyed budgeting: 'all the money went through her hands, and the household arrangements were guided by her will and pleasure' (*MB* 23). To some extent, her self-reliance is able to grow not just because of maternal absence, but *because* of her class position. She is a complete foil to the languid Carson daughters, who breathe in the atmosphere of conservatory flowers whilst listlessly turning over a parcel of sheet music. When Mary needs to act, to fetch Will, she finds an enormously powerful, and untapped, inner strength: 'with the call upon her exertions, and her various qualities of judgement and discretion, came the answering consciousness of innate power to meet the emergency' (*MB* 289). She is embellished with language which links her in with male chivalric literary tradition, being compared to one 'who discovers the silken clue which guides to some bower of bliss, and secure of the power within his grasp, has to wait for a time before he may thread the labyrinth' (*MB* 298–9). Selflessly, she takes on the role of justice: 'She longed to do all herself; to be his liberator, his deliverer; to win him life, though she might never regain his lost love by her own exertions' (*MB* 300). 'Normal' gender roles, of victim and liberator, are reversed. Nonetheless, Gaskell does not allow her heroine to remain in this triumphant state of energetic power: her exertions over, she falls sick with a form of brain fever. This seems a function of both psychological and narratological uncertainty: what to do in the case of a daughter who disobeys, as it were, her own father (for her actions do not just go against the patriarchal norm, but carry with them the potential to unmask her father as the perpetrator of the murder), and who also, perhaps, oversteps conventional bounds of female social activity. Mary's personal fate – married to Jem, mother of a son, starting a new life in a new country – is as much an avoidance of thinking through the implications inherent in having a powerful woman acting, to all intents and purposes, alone and from her own initiative, as it is an avoidance, a gesture of despair of actually doing much about the problems of industrial Manchester.

The ending is by no means the only point of apparent uncertainty in the book. The narrative voice itself is continually issuing disclaimers, from the Preface onwards: 'I know nothing of Political Economy, or the theories of trade' (*MB* xxxvi). Later we are told, in relation to the circumstances which led to the workers' strike: 'I am not sure if I can express myself in the technical terms of either masters or workmen, but I will try simply to state the case on which the latter deliberated' (*MB* 200). At one level, such utterances may be read as a form of winning feminine modesty, designed to counter potential accusations of presumption at a woman writer's venturing beyond her allocated sphere. At another, they may be seen as symptomatic of one of the novel's underlying themes: the greater power achieved by stimulating the emotions, of appealing to the 'heart's piety', over 'speechifying'. The deliberate destabilizing of the author's voiced 'authority' is counterbalanced by a careful manipulation of the reader to a position where no concrete solutions to social problems may be offered, but a model which stresses the importance of two-sided communication – between characters, between classes, between author and reader – is established.

3

Ruth

In *Mary Barton*, Elizabeth Gaskell uses the figure of Esther, Mary's aunt, not just to suggest the pressures which can force a woman into prostitution – the need for money with which to feed her sick daughter, in Esther's case – but to make a plea for understanding this category of woman: 'To whom shall the outcast prostitute tell her tale? Who will give her help in the day of need? Hers is the leper-sin, and all stand aloof dreading to be counted unclean' (*MB* 185).

Gaskell provided an immediate answer to her apparently rhetorical questions in the short story 'Lizzie Leigh' (1850), which centres round a young prostitute rescued by her country mother. Despite stressing the power of *one* maternal bond, however, Gaskell apparently found it necessary – perhaps for reasons of propriety, perhaps for reasons of pathos – to kill off Lizzie's illegitimate daughter. *Ruth*, her next novel, published early in 1853, dealt directly with a closely linked social question, the bearing of an illegitimate child, albeit to a woman who in no way could be thought of as a professional prostitute. To some extent, though, *Ruth* was probably directly prompted by discussion concerning prostitution. In 1850, Gaskell's Manchester friend W. R. Greg published an article entitled 'Prostitution' in the *Westminster Review*, in which he laments that 'no ruler or writer has yet been found with the nerve to face the sadness, the resolution to encounter the difficulties' of tackling this subject. Both writer and audience are implied when he claims that 'it is discreditable to a woman to know of their existence'. In this article, Greg stresses the 'pure unknowingness' of young girls who are led on, unwittingly, by more knowing seducers. He emphasizes social double standards, and elaborates on the theme of 'Lizzie Leigh', that the prodigal son inevitably meets with far more sympathetic treatment than the prodigal daughter. Notwithstanding, he helps to consolidate the dominant narrative of the 'fallen woman' who, having taken her first fatal step, inevitably faces an 'appalling doom'. The plot of Gaskell's novel only partly challenges the inevitability of this narrative in itself: however, the reader's response is manipulated to ensure that we query the justice inherent in assuming such inevitability.

Like *Mary Barton*, the outline of *Ruth* appears to owe a good deal to improbable narrative devices. Bellingham, the young gentleman who seduces Ruth whilst she is working as a seamstress, leaves her, pregnant. She's taken in by a Unitarian minister and his sister, who have her pose as a widow in their town. She becomes a governess/companion to a local industrialist's family, and then with a remarkable stroke of bad luck her former lover turns up as the new local MP, the industrialist's favoured candidate. This seems an unlikely incident of ill-fortune, but has similarities to an actual case about which Gaskell wrote to Dickens in 1850, involving a woman called Pasley, who had herself been a dressmaker's apprentice, was seduced by her own doctor, forced to turn to a career of petty crime, and, in prison, was confronted by her seducer, now the prison surgeon. In the novel, by another stroke of coincidence, the industrialist comes to learn of Ruth's past, and dismisses her out of his family's sight. She obtains employment as a private nurse, a career for women in which Gaskell was interested even before Florence Nightingale's efforts made it a respectable job for a middle-class woman. Typhoid fever – described in quasi-biblical terms as a creeping, terrible pestilence (Gaskell thus avoids running the risk of diffusing the social focus of this novel by too precise a depiction of urban squalor) – spreads from the Irish lodging houses in the town to all areas and classes: Ruth becomes a local heroine in her indefatigable caring for others. Her ultimate gesture comes in nursing Bellingham through the fever: he survives, but she succumbs herself. Mr Benson, the minister, is too overcome to preach a sermon at her funeral: he reads, instead, the promise of peaceful redemption from *Revelations 7*. Her son, Leonard, is left to mourn over her simple grave, where he is joined by Mr Bradshaw, the industrialist, his eyes filled with tears, moved by the innate goodness of the woman he had earlier been too quick to condemn by conventional social standards.

The novel's publication caused controversy among critics and readers. Gaskell herself would not let her daughters read it until they were 18. ' "Deep regret" is what my friends here feel and express' (L 220), she writes in a letter: she knew two men who had 'burnt the 1st vol. of *Ruth* as so very bad... and a third has forbidden his wife to read it; they sit next to us in chapel and you can't think how "improper" I feel under their eyes' (L 223). Perhaps if they had carried on reading they would have felt differently, for Ruth seems, as even some contemporary critics noted, to suffer from an excessively intense conscience, and positively obsessive feelings of guilt and shame and penitence. Nonetheless, whilst the novel was disapproved of for a variety of reasons, one should also note its didactic effect – especially on Josephine Butler, whose subsequent work with prostitutes culminated in the repeal of the discriminatory Contagious Diseases Act in 1886. In her autobiography, Butler recounts the impact of the book's publication in Oxford, where her husband was a geography don.

> A pure woman, it was reiterated, should be absolutely ignorant of a certain class of evils in the world, albeit those evils bore with murderous cruelty on other women. One young man seriously declared that he would not allow his own mother to read such a book as that under discussion – a book which seemed to me to have a very wholesome tendency, though dealing with a painful subject. Silence was thought to be the great duty of all on such subjects.

There is, of course, a huge amount of caution in Gaskell's treatment. She presents, on the surface, her most idealized picture of Victorian womanhood when telling what is, ostensibly, her most controversial tale. She had, necessarily, an inherent difficulty in her subject matter: the unwritability, in the mid-Victorian period, in respectable fiction, of female sexuality; and this is something which only disruptively emerges in the novel through dreams, and through undeveloped patterns in the imagery, particularly when Bellingham turns up again against a backcloth of storm clouds and lashing rain. There are strong hints that Ruth has to fight down sexual attraction with a stronger moral sense: her most powerful desire is given a maternal basis, as she passionately wishes to protect her son from contact with such a man as he. The suggestion that female sexuality exists, but yet is not a decisive factor in Ruth's 'fall' is a particularly interesting one, since in most contemporary writing – both fiction and nonfiction – which dealt with the 'problem' of the seduced woman, such a woman is presented either as the innocent victim of forces beyond her control, or else as guilty of overtly sexual behaviour. Gaskell's heroine fits neatly into neither category. Rather, she is continually associated with nature, whether she is presented noticing the painted wreaths of flowers on the walls of the house where she is employed as a seamstress; or leaving her old home, 'tearing off in a passion of love whole boughs of favourite China and damask roses, late flowering against the casement-window of what had been her mother's room' (R 38); or as being crowned with water-lilies when she and Bellingham go off to Wales. In such a context, Ruth's own beauty seems a further form of naturalness, but although she may be unconscious of its implications, the novel makes it very clear that within a social context, woman's beauty is a commodity, not just a 'natural' asset. Nature is something which carries positive connotations throughout the book, and Ruth's unquestioning responsiveness to it is stressed so insistently that a tricky problem is posed: if her behaviour itself has been 'natural', why is it regarded as a matter for guilt? Gaskell's text makes one query, however, whether it is possible for 'nature' to exist outside of social and cultural formations.

Although Gaskell may have overstated her case in making Ruth so penitent and pious, this novel is important as the first major piece of Victorian fiction to treat the theme of the 'fallen woman' not just with full compassion and sympathy, but through suggesting that she may be integrated into an English community, may indeed be 'respectable'. She is not denied entrance, like the daughter in Richard Redgrave's painting of 1851, *The Outcast*, or shipped off by the author to Australia, like Dickens's Little Em'ly, or Hetty, in George Eliot's *Adam Bede* (1859), or Nelly, the seduced woman in Eliza Meteyard's *Lucy Dean; the Noble Needlewoman* (*Eliza Cook's Journal*, 1850). Ruth both rises above her own weaknesses, gaining self-reliance – in the early part of the novel, she repeatedly gives way to 'passionate sorrow' and sinks into inaction – and she also rises above those members of the community who wish to condemn her. And it is not just Ruth's endeavours that are seen to be important, but the fact that she is helped by people round her: Benson, his sister Faith, and their practical servant Sally, provide necessary exempla of compassion and Christian charity. They are surrogate parents, unlike Ruth's first employer, Mrs Mason, who failed to exercise 'tender vigilance and maternal care' over her young charges.

Moreover, Ruth's 'fall', or rather people's knowledge of it, is used as a catalyst through which others can learn moral lessons. Faith learns to suppress her initial moral doubts through the example of Ruth's goodness and humility. Jemima Bradshaw is forced to confront a thorny set of questions in relation to Ruth. She is initially quick to condemn her when she learns what her past has been, partly because she fears for the influence Ruth may have on her younger sisters, partly because her own comfortable sense that she lives in a secure world has been shattered. As in *Mary Barton*, Gaskell uses the language of myth and melodrama to register the impact of the shock:

> The diver, leaving the green sward, smooth and known, where his friends stand with their familiar smiling faces, admiring his glad bravery – the diver, down in an instant in the horrid depths of the sea, close to some strange, ghastly, lidless-eyed monster, can hardly more feel his blood curdle at the near terror than did Jemima now. Two hours ago – but a point of time on her mind's dial – she had never imagined that she should ever come into contact with anyone who had committed open sin; she had never shaped her conviction into words and sentences, but still it was *there*, that all the respectable, all the family and religious circumstances of her life, would hedge her in, and guard her from ever encountering the great shock of coming face to face with vice. (*R* 323)

But Jemima soon recognizes that in fact she had never observed the slightest glimpse of a stain on Ruth's character. This has far-reaching, unsettling implications, with which the reader is implicitly invited to share: 'Who was true? Who was not? Who was good and pure? Who was not? The very foundations of Jemima's belief in her mind were shaken' (*R* 323) – or rather, one might say, she is learning that it is important not to judge according to preconceptions and stereotypes. Thus she arrives at the conclusion: 'whatever Ruth had been, she was good, and to be respected as such, now' (*R* 327).

Ruth may, in many ways, be an implausibly sweet heroine, but Gaskell exaggerates in order to make what were, for the time, a set of fictionally daring points. Moreover, the reader is left to draw the final conclusions. Benson's planned funeral sermon remains unpreached; the headstone to her grave uninscribed; Leonard's blank statement of grief to Bradshaw – 'My mother is dead, sir' (*R* 458), demands our internalization of the emotion behind according to the pattern established by the inadequate articulations of loss which Wordsworth offered up in the *Lyrical Ballads*. To some extent, Ruth's funeral sermon had already been preached by Benson to Bradshaw, when the latter attacks him for having 'stoop[ed] to deceit and imposition' in passing Ruth off as a widow, and someone fit to be a companion to his daughters. 'Is it not time', Benson asks:

> to change some of our ways of thinking and acting? I declare before God, that if I believe in any one human truth, it is this – that to every woman, who, like Ruth, has sinned, should be given a chance of self-redemption – and that such a chance should be given in no supercilious or contemptuous manner, but in the spirit of the holy Christ. (*R* 351)

Benson is led into self-questioning as a result of having told those necessary white lies which ensured that Ruth could have some form of social rehabilitation, and, perhaps even more importantly, regain her self-respect. His excusable mendacity is noncommittally juxtaposed by Gaskell with what are conspicuously more reprehensible forms of falsehood in the public world: the bribery which almost certainly guaranteed that Bellingham was elected as MP, and the forgery which Bradshaw finds that his own son was practising.

The disadvantage of overplaying Ruth's virtues was, however, as W. R. Greg pointed out in 'The False Morality of Lady Novelists' (*National Review*, 1859), that by giving us such a pure and unselfish character, by giving such 'faultless' reasons for her lapse from chastity, and by 'affirming that the sin committed was of so deep a dye that only a life of atoning and enduring persistence would wipe it out', Ruth had no representative status: she could not be considered as one of 'the ordinary class of betrayed and deserted Magdalens'. She hardly seems in need of 'self-redemption', even to the Victorian reader.

On the surface, Gaskell can fairly be accused of overcompensating for the shockingness of her subject matter. From this perspective, Ruth's death may be read as a capitulation to the orthodoxy that in at least middle-class mid-Victorian fiction, and indeed, in nonfictional narratives, the 'fallen woman' is better off – ultimately – dead. That a fallen woman would inevitably end in river or gutter was a potent myth, suggesting that once she had strayed, a woman was almost inevitably severed from her original community. Little distinction was actually made between the woman once seduced, and the career of a prostitute: one, frequently enough, in popular assumption if not in reality, led to the other. Such a myth informs Bellingham's thinking when he arrives at Bradshaw's seaside holiday house, and notes the remarkable resemblance of the governess to Ruth. He does not believe that it could be Ruth herself, although he wonders 'what had become of her; though, of course, there was but one thing that could have happened, and perhaps it was as well he did not know her end, for most likely it would have made him very uncomfortable' (R 278). However, Gaskell herself acknowledged that the controversy which *Ruth* provoked meant that the topic of the 'fallen woman' was, at least temporarily, not brushed aside with the ease with which Bellingham had tried to banish it. The book had made people 'talk and think a little on a subject which is so painful that it requires all one's bravery not to hide one's head like an ostrich and try by doing so to forget that the evil exists' (L 227).

Yet Gaskell is more subtle than at first appears in the effects she achieves by killing off Ruth. First, her demise, however unmerited in some respects, is the logical fulfilment of certain narrative strands within the novel. It may be taken as having symbolic value, and not only because it seems to be taking her into a happier world than that which she has known, as a reward for the stoicism with which she's born her mental suffering, as well as for her more tangible efforts within the community. The circumstances of her death provide a means of dramatizing the irredeemably contaminating effects of men like Bellingham – and, for that matter, the dangers of their fascination: Ruth's precise motives for engaging in the potentially suicidal act of nursing him remain, at the very least, open to question.

Moreover, this death is a triumphal rather than a miserable one, and hence functions as a celebration first of Ruth's life, and then of the major force for which she comes to stand in the novel, the spiritual and redemptive power of motherhood. Believing in the value of this is the gamble taken by the minister, Mr Benson, when he first proposes that Ruth should come and live with him and his sister. Faith regards the coming fruits of Ruth's pregnancy in conventional terms: 'the badge of her shame' (*R* 119). He, on the other hand, draws a clear distinction: 'The sin appears to me to be quite distinct from its consequences', a division which Gaskell herself upholds, whilst showing, of course, that many within the community damagingly do not. Moreover, continues Benson, the baby will, through the responsibilities of motherhood, bring a benefit with it: 'If her life has hitherto been self-seeking, and wickedly thoughtless' (not that, of course, this *has* been the case, but Benson shows his spiritual generosity through imagining the worst possible position):

> here is the very instrument to make her forget herself, and be thoughtful for another. Teach her (and God will teach her, if man does not come between) to reverence her child; and this reverence will shut out sin, – and will be purification. (*R* 119)

One could argue that, in practice, Ruth's devotion to little Leonard might have proved to be damagingly claustrophobic to the growing boy, but this pre-Lawrentian problem is, in a sense, avoided by Ruth's death, and with his being taken on, having inherited an aptitude for compassionate caring, as a doctor's apprentice. The doctor himself quietly owns up to being illegitimate, Gaskell thus providing a nudging reminder that one's birth need not function as a disabling stigma. Leonard's education has been conducted by Ruth as a 'series of experiments' (*R* 202) aimed at encouraging 'self-dependence'; the fact that he is a 'law unto himself' (*R* 383) is no sign of dangerous wilfulness, but, in Unitarian terms, a desideratum of education: Gaskell uses the same phrase approvingly, in a letter, about one of her own daughters. Unmistakably, though, it's Ruth's motherhood, and concern for her son, which gives not just strength but purpose and continuity to her life.

It is a mark of Gaskell's success in convincing her readers of Ruth's worth that she should have aroused protest by killing her off. Many, like Elizabeth Barrett, found the ending unduly sacrificial on Gaskell's part. Charlotte Brontë, reading an outline of the novel which Gaskell sent her before the full text was written, demanded:

> Yet – hear my protest!
> Why should she die? Why are we to shut up the book weeping?

My heart fails me already at the thought of the pang it will have to undergo. And yet you must follow the impulse of your own inspiration. If *that* commands the slaying of the victim, no bystander has a right to put out his hand to stay the sacrificial knife: but I hold you a stern priestess in such matters.

Yet despite the symbolic force of Ruth's 'good death', one might also plausibly argue that the dissatisfaction which so many readers, contemporary and modern, have felt at the conclusion of the novel – the regret that Ruth should have to be sacrificed – is, in fact, a response which may carry with it an effective didactic purpose. For the Victorian reader, at least, it called into question the desire that the narrative of the 'fallen woman' should necessarily have such a predictable ending. Rather than being a conventional gesture, this ending uses the reader's response of feeling cheated or bereft to challenge the assumptions which lie behind such conventions.

4

Story-telling and *Cranford*

In a letter, Charles Dickens called Elizabeth Gaskell his 'dear Scheherezade', after the story-teller in *The Arabian Nights* who tells a compulsively fascinating string of stories in order to forestall the revengeful execution of herself and other women. 'I am sure,' he wrote, 'your powers of narrative can never be exhausted in a single night, but must be good for at least a thousand nights and one.' Gaskell was an inveterate story-teller: her letters are full of anecdotes; she delighted in gossip about people she knew (and picked up and passed on little anecdotes about people she didn't). Her output as a whole dramatizes the heterogeneity of women's histories, of their modes of narrating them, and of the challenges that a woman's viewpoint – or set of viewpoints – might pose to dominant male conventions.

Her short stories and novellas range over periods, places and genres. In some, she tries out themes which are developed at greater length in her novels. For example, in a very early story, 'The Sexton's Hero' (1847, published in the radical *Howitt's Journal*), she interrogates the concept of heroism, locating it in loyalty and endurance rather than in grandiose ideas of public, particularly military, duty. It is, the narrator asserts, a 'poor, unchristian heroism, whose manifestation consists of injury to others!' (*CPT* 317). According to such a system of values, there is more heroism in Jem rescuing his father from a blaze, in *Mary Barton*, than in all Charley Kinraid's naval successes in *Sylvia's Lovers*. The short stories necessarily question any idea that heroism or nobility of action might be a male prerogative. Susan Dixon, in 'Half a Lifetime Ago', loses Michael, the man who had promised to marry her. She herself had sworn to her dying mother that she would look after her young brother, the 'feeble' Willie, a Wordsworthian Idiot Boy, and Michael is not prepared to

29

take on this compassionate charge. Yet years later, Susan attempts to rescue Michael after he has fallen and died from exposure in the snow: she then extends her capacity for love and practical help to his widow and children, who come to live in her home.

Elsewhere, Gaskell pursues her fascination, as in *Ruth* and *North and South*, with the idea of the 'necessary' lie, and with the impossibility of keeping the past hidden. Ellinor Wilkins, in 'A Dark Night's Work' (1863), spends eighteen years backing up her father's lies after he kills his clerk, yet, as she recognizes, 'I always knew it must be found out' (*DNW* 161). Not all her recurrent themes receive familiar treatment, however. In 'The Manchester Marriage' (1858), the sailor home from the sea finds his wife happily remarried: his only option (unlike the more resourceful, if less steadfast Charley Kinraid) is suicide. In other tales, such as 'The Old Nurse's Story' (1852) and 'The Crooked Branch' (1859), Gaskell pursues her interest in the strange and the supernatural. She also explores a wider historical and geographical range than in her novels: 'Lois the Witch' (1859) is set during the Salem witch-hunt of 1692. Lois, fulfilling her mother's dying wish that she seek out her emigrant uncle, finds herself entrapped by the desires and jealousies of her new-found relatives; by her own past – she was cursed by a drowning witch when a child – and by the need of the fearful to have sacrificial scapegoats. One of the most unusual of Gaskell's stories, and most deliberately self-conscious of all her pieces of writing, is 'Curious if True' (1860), in which the narrator, searching for his ancestors in France, turns up at the archetypal fairy-story castle in a dense wood, with 'pepper boxes, and *tourelles* and what not fantastically going up into the dim starlight' (*CP* 243). It is populated with a range of fairy-tale characters, from a grey whiskered Puss-in-Boots to Bluebeard. They recount their life-histories to him, and, for most of its course, the tale seems no more than a *jeu d'esprit* at the expense of one who does not realize that, since his name is Richard Whittingham, he is part of this legendary world and thus it is no surprise that these bizarre characters should have some acquaintance with his own doings – even with his cat. Yet this playfulness leads up to a more serious dénouement which links 'Curious if True' back to Gaskell's social and political concerns. For this particular self-made man half overhears a snatch of conversation concerning a Utopian future:

'Then everybody would have their rights, and we should have no more trouble. Is it not, monsieur?', addressing me.

'If I were in England, I should imagine madame was speaking of the reform bill, or the millennium – but I am in ignorance.' (CP 256)

At the entrance of the Fairy Godmother, Whittingham awakes, thus leaving the reader to wonder whether the idea of political and social justice can only exist in a fairy-tale world.

Many of Gaskell's novels contain interpolated narratives, which sometimes function (as in *Mary Barton*, when Job Leigh tells how he and his friend carried the baby Margaret back from London after her mother's death) to amplify our sense of characters' pasts as well as to reinforce major themes in the novel: in this case the fact that caring is not a maternal prerogative. Or they may operate as parables: Sylvia's mother, in *Sylvia's Lovers*, warns her daughter about the girl she knew when she was a child, who after falling passionately in love with a man who deserted her, pined and moped, and eventually turned mad. *My Lady Ludlow* (1858) provides Gaskell's most notable example of a story-within-a-story, when Lady Ludlow recounts to Margaret Dawson (in turn relating her life-history to a circle of friends) the moving and dramatic tale of Clémont and Virginie, aristocratic lovers at the time of the French Revolution who are betrayed by the son of Virginie's concierge and guillotined. Lady Ludlow does this in order to make a point about the inadvisability of educating servants to read and write, something which in turn – like the content of the story itself – signals her resistance to change.

Cranford (1853) is the work in which Gaskell most conspicuously spins one tale after another. This is partly the result of its mode of publication: it grew from a couple of pieces in which she recollected life in Knutsford, 'The Last Generation in England' (1849) and 'Mr Harrison's Confessions' (spring 1851), followed by what she initially thought would be a one-off piece, 'Our Society at Cranford', published in Dickens's magazine *Household Words* late in 1851. The Cranford episodes continued in *Household Words* until May 1853. On the surface, *Cranford* presents a quaint picture of provincial life; a gynocentric life since, we are told in the first sentence, it is a society of 'Amazons'. Throughout, however, a somewhat ironic distance from this society is maintained, and hence the work functions as a critique of the growing mid-nineteenth-century trend of nostalgia for a vanishing way of life.

The fierceness of these women lies in fact in little more than attempting to keep up appearances, and in never openly admitting to straightened circumstances. Rather, they practise 'elegant economy' (C 3) and observe minute rules of etiquette – at the tea-table, in the wearing of appropriate headgear, in keeping to well-understood patterns of social visiting – in order to safeguard their lifestyle. Self-respect dependent upon a reticence concerning one's feelings is as important as status, so Mary, the narrator, learns of the great sadness in her friend Miss Matty's life more through what she fails to tell her than through the details she reveals. More than any other of Gaskell's works, *Cranford* was responsible for establishing her reputation, in the early decades of the twentieth century, as a 'feminine' writer, characterized by tact and by a devotion to domesticity.

But *Cranford* is no cosy portrayal of a society which has had a preservation order slapped upon it. Certainly, Gaskell shows a discriminating eye for whimsical detail: the newspapers spread on a smart new carpet to protect it from sunbeams or the passage of visitors' feet; the lace which had been soaking in milk to clean it, and was swallowed by the cat and forcibly regurgitated, its wearer always proud to announce that it had been 'in Pussy's inside' (C 79); Miss Pole, who confuses the great Lama of Thibet with 'llamas, the beasts of burden' (C 112); the maid who sews red flannel in the shape of a cross and wears it 'on her inner garment' (C 105) as a precaution against the rumoured robbers. But just as Scheherezade told her stories to ward off execution, so the episodes also have a prophylactic function, their minutiae of detail seeming to ward off threats of the change and disruption of modern life. In the very first episode, Captain Brown is killed by a train. Such a train doubtless ran on tracks linking Cranford with Drumble, the industrial city where the narrator, Mary Smith, lives when not visiting the provincial town. Her urban origin helps to guarantee the combination of affection and deliberate distance in her tone. Drumble is a city of industry, of banking, and of commerce: a fact which is firmly brought home when Miss Matty's bank fails. Such an event demonstrates that Cranford society cannot actually exist as a self-contained microcosm, however much it may show a suspicion of strangers. Even the rumour of roving thieves 'occasioned as many precautions as if we were living among the Red Indians or the French' (C 90). Its xenophobic boundaries are challenged by Mary's imagination, too, when she muses on the miraculous process of inter-continental communication, and takes advantage of its possibilities. She posts a letter to a man in India she has every reason to believe is Peter, Miss Matty's long-lost brother, and 'it was gone from me like life – never to be recalled. It would get tossed about on the sea, and stained with sea-waves perhaps; and be carried among palm-trees, and scented with all tropical fragrance' (C 128). Even internal class barriers break down. Cranford's class stratification is contested when Lady Glenmire marries the local doctor, Mr Hoggins, who happily sups on bread and cheese and beer.

To imagine that one can be self-contained is an illusion: strength, in this novel, lies in social solidarity. This is most strongly seen when Miss Matty loses her money: the other ladies of Cranford contribute what they can to set her up as a tea-seller and sweet-shop keeper – although, once again, Gaskell's irony is at work in showing that her kindly commercial practices would not enable her to survive elsewhere. As Mary comments: 'my father says; "such simplicity might be very well in Cranford, but would never do in the world"' (C 145). In respect of its marketing practices, Cranford might be responding imperfectly to change. But social forms are shown as mutating in other ways. Despite the stress which the Cranford ladies habitually place on the importance of class distinctions, it is in fact Miss Matty's loyal servant Betty and her new, labourer husband who offer her a home. The viability of this arrangement is not, in the end, put to the test, because Peter returns from India with enough money to bale out his sister. This act in turn exposes a further illusion held by the women of Cranford: that they can in fact manage without those awkward, incomprehensible, and superfluous creatures, men. *Cranford* is no proto-feminist fable in this respect: rather, Gaskell can be read as being somewhat tongue-in-cheek about the self-protective conversational and socializing characteristics of the unmarried woman.

But in many other ways, Elizabeth Gaskell is experimenting in this work with what might be thought of as women's narrative. Mary comments that:

> I had often occasion to notice the use that was made of fragments and small opportunities in Cranford; the rose-leaves that were gathered ere they fell, to make into a pot-pourri for some one who had no garden;

the little bundles of lavender-flowers sent to strew the drawers of some town-dweller, or to burn in the chamber of some invalid. (C 15)

Similarly, *Cranford* is made up of 'fragments and small opportunities', rather like the germs of stories which are found in the letters which Miss Matty has kept tied into bundles, and which she reads with Mary: letters which carried with them 'a vivid and intense sense of the present time, which seemed so strong and full, as if it could never pass away' (C 42–3) but which now symbolize, as they are dropped one by one into the fire, the passing of a changing world. Personal and social loss coalesce. Miss Matty's philosophy, that 'a little credulity helps one on through life very smoothly, – better than always doubting and doubting, and seeing difficulties and disagreeables in everything' (C 108) reads like an advertisement for the necessary and healthy distraction that may be provided by reading fiction, but the episodic way in which *Cranford* is narrated connects it with traditions of oral narrative. The role of Mary herself changes subtly as the work progresses: at first she is an amateur collector of episodes from the town she visits, interpreting its curiosities for an uninitiated readership ('Do you know what a calash is? It is a covering worn over caps, not unlike the heads fastened on old-fashioned gigs...' C 65). She becomes, however, increasingly active in shaping the story she records: initiating the scheme to set Miss Matty up in her tea-shop, and sending off the letter that recalls Peter.

As both local historian and a manipulator of events, Mary Smith occupies a unique narrative position. She is neither coyly self-effacing, like Dickens's Esther in *Bleak House*, nor deliberately self-deprecating, like Charlotte Brontë's Lucy Snowe in *Villette*. With her own name (albeit one which is synonymous with self-effacing ordinariness), she is manifestly a fiction, unlike the narrator in *Mary Barton*, whose first-person interventions encourage one to equate her presence and personality with that of the real author; but she is no Jane Eyre, whose story forms the focus of the novel she narrates. Her role is above all that of a mediating friend, linking the world of *Cranford* with the presumed knowledge and values of her readers. The sense of intimacy which is created is not dependent, as early critics would have it, on some form of innate femininity emanating from Gaskell's personality. Rather, as one can see by placing *Cranford* in the context of her other fictions, long

34

and short, with their varied narrative techniques, it is a bold creation of a woman's voice confident in her capacity to act as an objective social commentator.

5

North and South

North and South (1855) initially appeared, like *Cranford*, in serial form within *Household Words*. This was a mode of publication which Gaskell found constraining. She wrote to Anna Jameson in January 1855 that 'If the story had been poured just warm out of the mind, it would have taken a much larger mould. It was the cruel necessity of compressing it that hampered me' (*L* 330–1). Yet Dickens found the novel irritatingly diffuse, complaining, just after he had read the novel's seventh instalment, that 'Mrs. Gaskell's story, so divided, is wearisome in the last degree'. Certainly, it would not have been possible for the novel's original readers, encountering the progress of the heroine Margaret Hale number by number, to predict how the story was going to develop. Opening in London, *North and South* at first seems to be a tale of fashionable society; then, as Margaret's father announces that his beliefs no longer allow him to carry out conscientiously the duties of a Church of England parson, the novel appears to engage with issues of religious doubt. This was the impression which Charlotte Brontë, at least, carried away with her after finishing the fifth number, writing to her friend: 'I think I see the ground you are about to take as far as the Church is concerned; not that of attack on her, but of defence of those who conscientiously differ from her, and feel it a duty to leave her fold.' But the ground shifts again. With the removal of the Hale family to Milton, the novel's central preoccupation with industrial relations becomes increasingly clear: even so, the novel later geographically returns both to London, and to the village of Helstone where Margaret grew up. This topographical mobility emphasizes the fact that Gaskell is not dealing simply with a localized set of problems, but is raising questions of social responsibility which bear on the country as a whole, and on a whole range of human relations.

To some extent, *North and South* is a riposte to those critics and friends who thought, like W. R. Greg, that Gaskell had placed so much weight on the hardships of the working people in *Mary Barton* that she had failed to consider in enough detail the difficulties faced by their employers. A personal friend of the Gaskell family, and hence someone who knew what knowledge was available to her, Greg complained in the *Edinburgh Review* that, despite the merits of *Mary Barton*, 'it was... the more necessary to inform [the workers] (as numerous stoppages of wealthy firms might indeed readily bring home to their conviction) that their masters *do* suffer, and suffer most painfully, from those reverses and stagnation of trade which they imagine to fall solely on themselves'. He condemned what he called Gaskell's 'fatally false idea' that 'the poor are to look at the rich and not to themselves for relief and rescue'. On the surface, Gaskell seems to fall into line with this very position: 'I know,' she wrote in 1850, 'and have always owned, that I have represented *but one* side of the question, and no one would welcome more than I should, a true and earnest representation of the other side' (*L* 119). Responding to those critics who believed that she had shown a 'morbid sensibility to the condition of operatives', she voiced apprehension that she had perhaps gone too far in the earlier novel: 'No one can feel more deeply than I how *wicked* it is to do anything to excite class against class, and the sin has been most unconscious if I have done so' (*L* 67). As we shall see, however, there are many aspects of *North and South* which are potentially more challenging both to fictional expectations, and to contemporary analyses of social dynamics, than an overt favouring of working-class perspectives would provide.

In *North and South*, Gaskell is not insensitive, by any means, to conditions of work in the cotton-mills. This can be seen when Margaret befriends the Higgins family, an act which starts to reconcile her to living in Milton, since, significantly, it gives her 'a human interest' (*NS* 74) in the place. The dying daughter, Bessy, tells her what aggravates the consumption that is killing her – fluff:

> Little bits, as fly off fro' the cotton, when they're carding it, and fill the air till it looks all fine white dust. They say it winds round the lungs, and tightens them up. Anyhow, there's many a one as works in a

carding-room, that falls into a waste, coughing and spitting blood, because they're just poisoned by the fluff. (*NS* 102)

This is an insider's view, in direct contrast to the deliberately insensitive reaction shown by Dickens's Harthouse, in *Hard Times*, who jokingly describes the person he asks for directions in a mill-town as 'one of the working people; who appeared to have been taking a shower-bath of something fluffy, which I assumed to be the raw material'. It is a direct blast, too, at those commentators who, continuing the tradition of such late-eighteenth-century writers as Erasmus Darwin, persisted in seeing aesthetic beauty in industrial processes at the expense of understanding the human impact of working conditions. Cook Taylor, in his *Handbook of Silk, Cotton and Woollen Manufacturers* of 1843, could write of how the cotton is slipped from the cylinder which has removed it from the carding box by:

a slip of metal, finely toothed like a comb, which, being worked against the cylinder by means of a crank, beats or brushes off the cotton in a fine filmy fleece. The cloud-like appearance of the carded cotton, as it is brushed from the ... finishing cylinder by the crank and comb, is singularly beautiful; a breath seems to disturb the delicacy of its texture, and to the touch it is all but impalpable.

But concern with factory conditions – more concern, incidentally, than is directly shown in *Mary Barton* – only occupies a small section of *North and South*, where the point of view remains resolutely that of the middle classes, however graphically they may be informed of the experiences of others. In demonstrating in detail how Thornton – generally reckoned, in Milton, to be an honest, if direct and blunt employer – suffers from vicissitudes in trade which lie well outside his capacity to influence or control, Gaskell did go, her contemporaries thought, some way towards redressing the balance which had been tilted by the perceived biases of *Mary Barton*. She starts with Thornton's intrinsic qualities; his physical appearance establishes him in idealized heroic terms: a man for the present, yet with a type of beauty borrowed from a classical aesthetic paradigm. In his face:

the straight brows fell low over the clear, deep-set earnest eyes, which, without being unpleasantly sharp, seemed intent enough to penetrate into the very heart and core of what he was looking at. The lines in the face were few but firm, as if they were carved in marble, and lay principally about the lips, which were slightly compressed over a set of teeth so faultless and beautiful as to give the effect of sudden sunlight when the rare bright smile, coming in an instant and shining out of the eyes, changed the whole look from the severe and resolved expression of a man ready to do and dare everything, to the keen honest enjoyment of the moment, which is seldom shown so fearlessly and instantaneously except by children. (*NS* 80)

This man is no effete, predatory Harry Carson or Henry Bellingham. Nor does he fit any bluff stereotype of the self-made industrialist, unlike Carlyle's figure of inventor/mill-owner in *Chartism*: 'Richard Arkwright, it would seem, was not a beautiful man; no romance-hero with haughty eyes, Apollo-lip and gesture like the herald Mercury, a plain almost gross, bag-cheeked, pot-bellied Lancashire man'.

Re-viewing social conditions was not just a matter of altering the perspectives from which the reader might see urban life. Gaskell redressed the balance of her two earlier novels in more ways than one. The vein of nostalgic pastoral, important to Gaskell's earlier work, even if coming under a certain amount of scrutiny in *Cranford*, is here partially suppressed by the picture given of agricultural working life. Polarity between north and south is promised not just by the novel's title, but by the opening chapters of the book, as Margaret moves from the 'village in a poem' (*NS* 12) of her youth and from her cousin's shallow social set in London to Milton. It is present, too, when Mr Hale addresses Thornton, saying that he 'would rather be a man toiling, suffering – nay, failing and successless – here, than lead a dull prosperous life in the old worn grooves of what you call more aristocratic society down in the South, with their slow days of careless ease' (*NS* 81). But, again, Margaret functions as a tool for the reader's education, breaking down the apparent geographical and social dichotomy. Experience of the industrial north enables her to give voice to her knowledge of agricultural labouring life. She tells the disillusioned northern workman, Higgins, who contemplates moving south in search of work, that:

You would not bear the dulness of the life; you don't know what it is; it would eat you away like rust. Those that have lived there all their lives, are used to soaking in the stagnant waters. They labour on, from day to day, in the great solitude of steaming fields – never speaking or lifting up their poor, bent, downcast heads. The hard spade-work robs their brain of life; the sameness of their toil deadens their imagination... (NS 306)

Subsequently, returning to London, the broadened perspective which life in the north has given her makes her fearful 'lest she should even become sleepily deadened into forgetfulness of anything beyond the life which was lapping her round with luxury. There might be toilers and moilers there in London, but she never saw them' (NS 373), and she chafes against this sense. When, late in the novel, she returns to her native Helstone, she initially mourns the demolition of the picturesque cottages which she used to sketch, the trimming and narrowing of the roadside, and the 'modernization' of her old home. But she draws a wider point from these alterations: 'After all it is right... If the world stood still, it would retrograde and become corrupt... Looking out of myself, and my own painful sense of change, the progress of all around me is right and necessary' (NS 400).

From naïvely equating mill-owners with the tradespeople she used to regard as being beyond the social pale ('I'm sure you don't want me to admire butchers and bakers, and candlestick-makers, do you, mamma?' NS 19), Margaret comes, eventually, to fall in love with Thornton. It is Margaret who works to achieve some kind of reconciliation and moving understanding between master and men, as typified by Thornton on the one hand, and Higgins on the other. She is, despite her occasional fainting fits, a notably active heroine. Rather like Mary Barton, metaphorically going into battle to defend Jem, she interposes herself between Thornton and an angry, rioting crowd:

> She had lifted the great iron bar of the door with an imperious force – had thrown the door open wide – and was there, in face of that angry sea of men, her eyes smiting them with flaming arrows of reproach... She threw her arms around him; she made her body into a shield from the fierce people beyond. (NS 178–9)

This occurs before any kind of romantic interest has grown up between them – at least, before it has become overtly established, for the structural juxtaposition of the two within the narrative certainly creates a sense of expectancy on the reader's part, strengthened by Mrs Thornton's protective apprehension that Margaret must inevitably be pursuing her son, and strengthened, too, by the suggestion of erotic passion which comes in this scene from the conjunction of sudden protective embrace and inflamed male violence. The resulting misinterpretation of her action, not least by Thornton's mother, turns out to be the least of the misunderstandings which Margaret has to endure.

For the industrial theme is subordinated to the melodramatically personal for much of the centre of the story. Frederick, Margaret's brother, exiled abroad on suspicion of having instigated a ship-board mutiny, slinks back into the country to visit their mother's death-bed: Thornton witnesses their touching parting at a railway station, and fears not just that Margaret loves another, but that she is even prepared to lie about her presence there – for she denies her presence to the curious police (Frederick pushed a man who threatened to reveal his identity, claim the reward, and condemn him to almost certain death from a yard-arm, and the man died from his injuries). Margaret's inability to defend her reputation to Thornton – to do so would be to endanger Frederick – serves to dramatize her personal strengths and to enhance the reader's impression of her capacity to make decisions independently, whilst it simultaneously ensures the tension of a deferred, and for a while increasingly unlikely, romantic conclusion.

North and South ends, like so much Victorian fiction, with the promise of a marriage, between, inevitably, Margaret and Thornton. The misunderstanding concerning Frederick is cleared up. The principal agent in this clarification is not, significantly, Margaret's father's close friend Mr Bell, who intends to set the record straight, but dies (leaving his fortune to Margaret) before he has the chance to do so. Rather, it is the working man, Higgins, who enlightens Thornton from the knowledge he picked up from his daughter who worked in the Hales's home. Whilst this quietly teaches that secrets cannot be kept, it also shows sympathy and confidence between the classes operating to personal advantage.

Once again, however, it is appropriate to emphasize Margaret's role as the more active partner in the eventual coupling of Thornton and herself. It is she who has taught him to exercise, in the public sphere, the 'womanly' quality of sympathy which allows him to become a desirably thoughtful employer – although one should note that in exercising 'influence' here she is doing no more than adopting what many commentators of the time considered to be woman's most appropriate role. Since Margaret

41

is a character who applies a standard of behaviour which does not differentiate between the sphere of the home and that of the workplace, it has been suggested that Gaskell is putting forward a kind of 'social maternalism' to replace traditional paternalistic values. The power of maternal influence is reinforced by Thornton's own family circumstances, to which Margaret refers when she accuses the employer of 'professing to despise people for careless, wasteful improvidence, without ever seeming to think it his duty to try to make them different – to give them anything of the training which his mother gave him, and to which he evidently owes his position' (NS 86).

At a more practical level, it is Margaret who, thanks to her inheritance, supplies the money which will enable Thornton to carry on his 'experiments' in humanizing industrial relations, 'beyond the mere "cash nexus"' (NS 431). As he explains:

> I have arrived at the conviction that no mere institutions, however wise, and however much thought may have been required to organize and arrange them, can attach class to class as they should be attached, unless the working out of such institutions bring the individuals of the different classes into actual personal contact. (NS 431–2)

The terms of this personal contact, however, have occasioned a good deal of critical debate. For North and South is ultimately equivocal about the viability of making an analogy between family relationships and those between masters and men. Even if social maternalism is put forward as a possible model for the future, one should note that the novel itself is suspicious about those who make parallels between industrial relations and family structures. The workers we encounter in the novel are, after all, adults. Relatively early in their association, Margaret repeats to Thornton (without disclosing her source) Higgins's injured feelings that 'the masters would like their hands to be merely tall, large children – living in the present moment – with a blind unreasoning kind of obedience' (NS 119), a viewpoint which Thornton answers by saying that he indeed considers his employees 'in the condition of children, while I deny that we, the masters, have anything to do with the making or keeping them so.' Nonetheless, since 'in our infancy we require a wise despotism to govern us', this is the stance he proposes to take, he initially says, at least so long as his workers are inside the gates of his factory. Gaskell offers a further gloss on the workplace/family analogy through Higgins's comment that 'Meddling 'twixt master and man is liker meddling 'twixt husband and wife than aught else' (*NS* 308): one can take from this the idea that it would be advisable for each partner to acknowledge, and come to understand, the differing, yet equally valid perspective of the other.

The model of the family, embodying, as it did, so many implications for most Victorian readers about 'natural' roles and power systems, suggests a form in which roles are relatively fixed – something we see uncritically presented in the familial and industrial relations in Dickens's *Hard Times*, which had appeared in *Household Words* shortly before *North and South*. The model appears to offer little in the way of possibility for alteration in underlying social structures. The trouble with the concept of social maternalism is that it still implies an inequality of power, even if this inequality is informed by love and sympathy. Moreover, within the context of the novel, we are offered a diverse range of mothers as potential models, which complicates any notion that the concept was an unproblematic one for Gaskell. Mrs Thornton may have brought up her son to respect the need to work for one's money and build carefully on one's assets, but her home is chilly and uninviting; her daughter Fanny insipid, no inheritor of her mother's strength. Mrs Hale needs support from Dixon, her maid, and from her daughter, Margaret, more than she can ever offer it to others. Mrs Shaw, Margaret's aunt, 'was as good-tempered as could be', a 'charming domestic quality' (*NS* 416), but is socially short-sighted, largely concerned, like Edith, her daughter, with the immediate upper-middle-class circle in which she moves.

So although Gaskell unquestioningly admires women's capacity for sympathy and understanding, which were characteristics commonly linked, in the mid-century, with her assumed destined role as mother, she is, in *North and South*, investigating the exercise of this capacity by equals in adult partnerships. She also considers that sympathy, like other conventionally gendered characteristics, may be wielded by members of either sex. Neither Margaret nor Thornton are entirely conventional according to the behavioural and psychological cultural norms of their time: each blends within him- or herself decisiveness, independence, pride, integrity, and irrational passionate feelings. Presuppositions about the degree of difference between women and men, like those concerning the degree of difference between North and South – and indeed, potentially, between members of differing classes – are thus called into question.

Unlike most of the heroines of Victorian fiction, Margaret does not accept that she must necessarily look for satisfaction within marriage. Before being reunited with Thornton, she reclaims 'her life into her own hands' (NS 416), and takes up social work, acknowledging a sense of responsibility towards herself that echoes, in the voicing of her self-rationalization, Gaskell's epistolary comments about the problems which beset her in organizing the priorities in her own life. She had learnt:

> that she herself must one day answer for her own life, and what she had done with it; and she tried to settle that most difficult problem for women, how much was to be utterly merged in obedience to authority, and how much might be set apart for freedom in working. (NS 416)

But if this glances towards an afterlife, it is not on a distanced outcome that North and South ultimately focuses. Whilst in Mary Barton and in Ruth Gaskell situated promises of happiness, whether heavenly or earthly, away from the immediate problems of England, this novel derives its strength from the way in which she suggests that the future lies in integrating private and public concerns at home, in a social and cultural context which, she emphasizes throughout the text, is, and will continue to be, in a state of change.

6

Sylvia's Lovers

Sylvia's Lovers (1863) is the gloomiest of all Gaskell's longer fictions: she herself called it 'the saddest story I ever wrote'. It is set at the time of the French Revolutionary Wars, in Monkshaven (Whitby) on the Yorkshire coast, and Gaskell worked hard to establish a sense of very precise locality, from delineating the exact topography of the expanding fishing-port, to rigorously recording all dialogue in the local dialect, something which many reviewers found wearisome. Had she not done this, however, one would have missed the juxtaposition of localized, domestic drama, with its suspicions, apprehensions, and tensions, with a period of national anxiety displaying identical characteristics. The forces of passion, violence, and revenge dissolve the boundaries between the two worlds.

The plot involves few major characters, but is convoluted. Each of the protagonists is caught in an emotionally charged set of relations. Sylvia is a farmer's daughter, courted by two men: her respectable, somewhat self-righteous cousin Philip, a draper's assistant, and the far more dashing Charley Kinraid, a 'specksioneer' – the chief harpooner on a whaling ship. Sylvia's preference for Kinraid is obvious, particularly to Philip, who is not just straightforwardly jealous, but worried that the speck-sioneer will treat Sylvia in as cavalier a fashion as he has been rumoured to behave towards other girls. On his way back to join his whaling ship, Kinraid is seized by the press-gang who roam the Yorkshire coast looking for promising sailors to carry off to fight against the French. Philip witnesses this abduction: Kinraid begs him to tell Sylvia what has happened and swears that he will be faithful to her, a message which Philip fails to deliver, letting Sylvia believe that her betrothed must have been drowned. This lie is not told for altruistic reasons, like those in *Ruth* and *North and South*: it is fundamentally a means of exercising power over Sylvia. Events initially seem to play into Philip's hands. Charley's sodden hat is found, and since no one else witnessed this particular press-gang raid, drowning would seem to be the only fate which could possibly have befallen him. Sylvia's own father is found guilty of inciting a riot against the press-gang tactics, and is executed; her mother falls ill, and, despondently, Sylvia marries Philip, partly to give her mother a home, partly out of a feeling of obligation for all he has done for her family. This captive, subdued Sylvia is not, of course, the Sylvia of Philip's desire. Indeed, he 'wanted the old Sylvia back again; captious, capricious, wilful, haughty, merry, charming. Alas! that Sylvia was gone for ever' (*SL* 330).

These personal dramas are paralleled by concerns in the wider world. The issues of trust, honesty, and responsibility, for example, crop up in Philip's professional life when the draper's owners, the Fosters (who entrust Philip and his colleague Coulson with a partnership whilst they pursue their banking activities), find that they have been lending money to a London silk-manufacturer in whom they had had confidence, but who was now rumoured to be going bankrupt. Sent to London, Philip pursues truth and justice meticulously: such rules prove harder to apply to his own life. Gaskell is elaborating on one of the themes of her previous novel: that a division between the terms in which one leads one's professional and one's private life is in fact inadvisable. Although it might be a good thing to compartmentalize aspects of one's life – as she had recently argued in *The Life of Charlotte Brontë* – the recurrence of this theme suggests her need to stress that there must be no *moral* disjuncture between these separate parts.

The question of responsibility and obligations runs through the novel, from debates about the relationship between government and governed, to the often-emphasized need to show loyalty to kin. But again, anxiety about a pull towards disjuncture often surfaces, and mingled with this is a preoccupation with the fact that personal bias may prevent one from ever assessing situations clearly. Gaskell shows that the laws of God and man, of the country and of human feeling, may frequently run counter to one another. Moreover, subjective involvement, the pull of desire, may hinder an individual from fairly evaluating the merits and consequences of his or her actions. Thus the protagonists continually define themselves in relation to others, and, for that matter, continually complicate matters by reading their own desires and projected feelings into the responses of these others. Hester, another draper's assistant, and eventually partner, is quietly in love with Philip herself. The narrator remarks that her readiness to help Philip prepare a home for his new wife is 'a quiet little bit of unconscious and unrecognized heroism', on a par with Susan's actions in 'Half a Life-Time Ago'. 'She really ended by such a conquest of self that she could absolutely sympathize with the proud expectant lover, and had quenched all envy of the beloved, in sympathy with the delight she imagined Sylvia must experience when she discovered all these proofs of Philip's fine consideration and care' (*SL* 338). But since Sylvia, married in mourning, accompanied by her disconsolate mother, goes through the whole process in a state of 'heavy abstraction' (*SL* 339), this noble self-abnegation meets with no answering response. Early in the novel, after they have both attended the funeral of a sailor who had been killed when the press-gang boarded his ship – the occasion on which Sylvia and Kinraid first see each other – Philip is anxious 'to show his sympathy with Sylvia, as far as he could read what was passing in her mind; but how was he to guess the multitude of tangled thoughts in that unseen receptacle?' (*SL* 76). Whilst the novel's plot hinges on one particular act of conceal-ment, reprehensible if understandable, its emotional action is completely underpinned by the way in which thoughts and fancies lie hidden – sometimes deliberately concealed, sometimes unconsciously so – within individual minds. Gaskell is, in effect, experimenting with the implications of the disjuncture between the conscious and the unconscious mind.

Inevitably, Kinraid turns up again, and he, and Sylvia, learn that Philip betrayed him. Sylvia banishes her husband: he leaves the town in shame, and enlists. Kinraid, too, goes back to sea, leaving Sylvia with her and Philip's baby, and, in a coincidence reminiscent of the then popular sensation fiction, the two rivals meet again at the Siege of St Jean d'Acre, where Philip saves Kinraid's life, before being badly wounded himself. Returning to England, Philip slowly makes his way, a lonely, discharged, wounded soldier, like a figure from a Wordsworth poem, back to Monkshaven, where he lives in extreme poverty, lodging incognito with an elderly woman. An object of charity at the unknowing hand of his own daughter, he shortly afterwards rescues her from drowning. His identity is discovered, and Sylvia goes to him in a spirit of reconciliation – the fact that Kinraid married not long after last seeing her seems to have convinced her of the specksioneer's fickleness compared to Philip's steadiness. He, too, asks forgiveness. Such a reconciliation, however, only serves to drive home the novel's theme of missed opportunities, of desires that go unspoken or miss their mark, for Philip now 'lay-a-dying – his life ended, his battles fought, his time for "being good" over and gone – the opportunity, once given in all eternity, past' (SL 498).

The narration retreats from Sylvia: we only learn, in a retrospective final page, that she became a pale, sad woman, who died before her daughter was grown up. It is as though without forming the focus for rival suitors, she has no story left. Her daughter, left money by one of the Fosters, marries into their family, and emigrates. Thus there is no sense of continuity through generations, and those who are left in Monkshaven to recount their memories tell a travestied version of the facts:

> the memory of man fades away. A few old people can still tell you the tradition of the man who died in a cottage somewhere about this spot, – died of starvation while his wife lived in hard-hearted plenty not two good stone-throws away. This is the form into which popular feeling, and ignorance of the real facts, have moulded the story. (SL 502)

Giving voice to those whom historical process, as well as class or gender, has rendered speechless, Gaskell's task resembles that of Wordsworth in, say, 'Michael', telling of a recent past that has disappeared under the pressures of social change, and that also is in danger of being unrecognizably mutated through oral narratives. This process is akin to what Gaskell increasingly perceived as the distorting effects of gossip, an issue which she examines further in *Wives and Daughters*.

Gaskell is careful to remind us throughout that this story has a historical setting, when life was sparser, opportunities for travel and education more limited. She partly does this through the insertion of generalized comments, partly through the inclusion of vivid localized detail: noting the marigolds which grew in the cottage gardens 'the petals of which flavoured the salt-beef broth' (SL 4); the 'three-legged creepie-stools that were hired out at a penny an hour' (*SL* 15) to market women. Yet to some extent her remarks about the distance between past and present are ironic. 'It is astonishing to look back', she comments:

> and find how differently constituted were the minds of most people fifty or sixty years ago; they felt, they understood, without going through reasoning or analytic processes, and if this was the case among the more educated people, of course it was still more so in the class to which Sylvia belonged. (*SL* 318)

But this is a novel which directs the reader's attention to instinctive rather than reasoned emotions: feelings which are perennially difficult to explain or justify. That, in *Sylvia's Lovers*, is the prerogative of the narrator, standing back from her characters to show us what their subjectivity masks from themselves. This narrative demonstrates time and time again that the more emotionally involved one is in a situation, the more one's own sense of identity and self-worth is invested in a particular outcome, the less clear-sighted can one be. Although *Sylvia's Lovers* may be read as an attempt to interpret the past with informed hindsight, and the question of the part played by author's and readers' disturbing biases never arises except through implication, the novel nonetheless raises a number of issues that cannot satisfactorily be explained away with rationalizing.

A good number of these issues cluster around the figure of Sylvia, and around the responses of those who relate to her. In some ways, Sylvia herself is curiously passive. The novel's title positions her as potential object, rather than subject: the focus of male attention rather than a potentially active agent in her own right. We are continually made aware of her as an object of the male gaze. Just as Mrs Mason, the dressmaker in *Ruth*, knows that if she takes her prettiest girls along to the ball in order to mend any of the gowns which need repairs, they will function as a visual advertisement for her establishment, so, in *Sylvia's Lovers*, a woman's possession of beauty is linked to her commercial worth. When Sylvia accompanies her mother to Monkshaven market, 'it might have been thought that the doctors had prescribed a diet of butter and eggs to all the men under forty in Monkshaven... There were more customers than formerly for the fleeces stored in the wool-loft; comely young butchers came after the calf almost before it had been decided to sell it; in short, excuses were seldom wanting to those who wished to see the beauty of Haytersbank Farm' (*SL* 121).

Yet Sylvia chafes against this passive role. Action is what she craves, and lacks. In many respects, she is a study of entrapment, of frustrated energy; she may be read as a displacement of the frustrations of many middle-class women at the time that the novel was published. Charley Kinraid is attractive to her not just because of his reputation for bravery or his 'half-tender, half-jesting conversation' (*SL* 181), but because his stories, even his occupation, suggest a far wider perspective and set of adventurous possibilities to her than had been encompassed by her small orbit of farm and fishing town. He tells her 'of burning volcanoes springing out of icy southern seas'; she regrets that since 'in the specksioneer's tale the flames were peopled with demons, there was no human interest for her in the wondrous scene in which she was no actor, only a spectator' (*SL* 106). Kinraid certainly awakens restlessness in Sylvia: after his disappearance, even Philip's visits are welcome since he 'brought some change into the heavy monotony of her life – monotony so peaceful until she had been stirred by passion out of that content with the small daily events which had now become burdensome recurrences' (*SL* 270).

Sylvia is manifestly happier out of doors: she feels constrained when married to Philip and living in the town, missing 'the free open air, the great dome of sky above the fields' (*SL* 342); having to dress respectably and wear shoes every time she goes out of the front door. Motherhood, in this novel, is not presented as a crowning blessing, but, the narrator tells us, 'by-and-by, the time came when she was a prisoner in the house; a prisoner in her room, lying in bed with a little baby by her side' (*SL* 350). Action is very much a male province in *Sylvia's Lovers*. Hester's quiet and deep love for Philip is blindingly obvious to the reader, but never breaks through her Quaker modesty to show her feelings to their object. She is another study in mute, frustrated desire: even at the novel's close, a twist of the plot robs her of the chance to be the agent of Philip's and Sylvia's reconciliation.

Yet if the chance for an active life is presented from one perspective as enviable, from another it is made to look like aggression. Once again, Gaskell's ambivalences regarding activity and femininity surface. With the exception of the young women who are roused to animal anger, like a chorus of Greek furies, when their men are seized by the press-gang (a response echoed in Sylvia's defiant expression – a 'helpless fury' (*SL* 280) – when the constables come to arrest her father), aggressive impulses are invariably masculine. Moreover, they are linked to what Gaskell shows to be a competitive struggle for personal survival and social furtherment. Such survival depends on the opportunistic exploitation of the circumstances in which one finds oneself, and its prime exponent is Charley Kinraid, unequivocally the most sexualized, and the most sexually self-conscious, of all the men in the book. Initially, he is placed in the world of whaling, where 'he might rise by daring and saving to be a shipowner himself' – numbers around him had done so, 'and this very fact made the distinction between class and class less apparent' (*SL* 7). Such initiative, although Gaskell leaves her readers to draw the parallel themselves, is similar to that which made Thornton, even Mr Carson, succeed as self-made businessmen. Kinraid fights savagely against his capture by the press-gang, but the same bravery and brightness which had ensured his mastery and reputation as a whaler enable him to turn his enforced naval career into a means of considerable personal advancement. He may indeed be devastated to learn that Sylvia has married Philip, but he does not mope over this, and relatively soon marries a pretty and charming Bristol heiress. The reader is no more able to feel resentful of this woman than is Sylvia, since the new Mrs Kinraid visits her to thank her with genuine warmth for her husband's bravery in saving Kinraid's life in battle.

Sylvia's Lovers is a novel which poses some troubling questions. It queries not just the steadfastness of human love and desire, but whether emotional fidelity, carried past a certain point, is self-destructive. It weighs up the claims of rationality – necessary, as we have seen, in avoiding self-delusion in relationships – against a rather uncertain hope in celestial futurity which, through the references to the Book of Revelations and the epigraph from Tennyson's *In Memoriam* ('Oh for thy voice to soothe and bless!/ What hope of answer, or redress?/ Behind the veil! Behind the veil!') seems to be all that is on offer to save the reader from pessimism. More disquietingly still, Gaskell implicitly interrogates the relationship between the presence of grief and loss – the emotional qualities which pervade the final part of the novel –

and the existence of any underlying divine ameliorative plan, such as the Unitarians believed in. This was, of course, a particularly pertinent question in the light of the social and theological debates sparked off by the publication of Darwin's *On The Origin of Species* (1859) and the controversial volume of theological pieces, *Essays and Reviews*, which appeared in 1860.

No confident answer to the problem of emotional pain is offered in *Sylvia's Lovers*; no theological consolation is proffered. Barriers between the differing spheres of public and private action are broken down by the themes and structure of this novel, but not with any resulting hope of individual improvement or social unification. Kinraid's social climbing may appear to provide the important exception, but he is hardly a character towards whom we are encouraged to feel great sympathy. The ruling principles of the future, this historically set novel suggests – in other words, the ruling principles of Gaskell's own time – will be those of strategy and survival. Whether they are to be welcomed is a different matter.

7

Cousin Phillis and Wives and Daughters

Superficially, *Wives and Daughters* seems a much quieter novel than its predecessors. Like the novel which Gaskell published immediately before it, *Sylvia's Lovers*, it is in some measure a historical novel: Gaskell returns to the 1820s and early 1830s, and to the same kind of provincial society that she depicted in *Cranford*. There is no hint of the growing industrial world; no juxtaposition of domestic drama with the emotions and actions of the Revolutionary Wars (apart from a lingering xenophobic feeling towards the French), nor any hints of the rick-burning and other agrarian outbursts of unrest at the time, which, in their turn, like the anti-press-gang riots, were to feed into the popular radicalism of the cities.

But *Wives and Daughters* is not a nostalgic novel. In it, Gaskell critically re-examines some of the themes which had been important to her throughout her writing career: the relationship between mother and child; questions of concealment and deception, and the socially revealing nature of closely observed detail. To this end, she builds on a new and forward-looking topic, hinted at in the underlying preoccupations of *Sylvia's Lovers*: the significance of Darwinian science, and its relationship to social change.

Social change forms the pivot of another work, which Gaskell wrote between the two longer novels: *Cousin Phillis*. In this, the young railway engineer Paul pays visits to some of his relatives, who live on a farm: a dissenting minister, and his wife and daughter. Phillis, the daughter, is kept in a state of protected childhood: a rehearsal, to some extent, of the theme of Mr Gibson's reluctance that his daughter Molly is growing up in

Wives and Daughters. But in the shorter work, the sense of Phillis Holman's family being caught in a time-warp is made the stronger by the simplicity and piety of the rural life they lead. Paul soon comes to regard Phillis more as a sister than as a potential romantic attachment: not so his co-worker Holdsworth. Holdsworth observes her, admires her, casts her into passive roles, as a goddess of nature, Sleeping Beauty, the subject of his sketch. An unmissable career opportunity for Holdsworth suddenly comes up, and this male intruder into the quiet world of the Holman family leaves for Canada, telling Paul, 'I shall come back like a prince from Canada, and waken her to my love' (*CP* 315).

Unfortunately, Phillis has already been awakened into feeling for Holdsworth: he has been over-idealizing 'her high tranquillity, her pure innocence' (*CP* 315). When she is clearly pining and sickening at his absence, Paul tells her that the engineer loved her, and plans to return. The reader, like Paul, is left wondering whether this would have been a secret best kept to himself. Phillis undoubtedly rallies, only to be precipitated into a brain-fever when she learns that Holdsworth has got married in Canada. She recovers, but only in an extremely subdued state. Two juxtaposed points are made by this tale: that the intrusion of the outside world, in the shape of mechanical engineers, is destructive; and yet that it is inevitable, like the spread of the railways they bring with them. One cannot hope to preserve the past in aspic, any more than the Holmans should presume that they can incarcerate their daughter in childhood for ever. Adulthood, however, brings deep sorrow for Phillis.

Or so it does in the printed version, completed by Gaskell with the editor of the *Cornhill*, George Smith, pressing her for copy and a conclusion. Her original intention was to show Phillis as an older, stronger, but still single woman, draining the land around the farm in accordance with the drawings which Holdsworth had left behind him, and having adopted some orphan children of her own. Gaskell's theme of the courage to be found in resignation, and the forgetting of individual sorrow in caring for others, would thus have been reasserted once again, but it was thwarted, apparently, by the demands of her magazine publisher. Nonetheless, the tone of Paul, who narrates *Cousin Phillis*, is itself one of nostalgic retrospection, and grief for his part in shattering the self-enclosed world of the Holmans. His first-person narration (the assumption of the sensitive masculine voice is yet another of Gaskell's experiments in narrative technique), and his over-whelming sense of reprehensible personal involvement masks him, however, to what is clear to the reader: the inevitability of social change, and the need to accommodate oneself to its implications.

The Darwinian figure of *Wives and Daughters*, the protagonist thus most overtly associated with forces of change, is Roger Hamley, younger son of Squire and Lady Hamley. But unlike *Cousin Phillis*, the longer novel does not adopt a male focus of consciousness, but returns to a fictional world seen largely from women's perspectives. The primary form of disruption is again the intrusion of outsiders into a previously secure domestic unit; an effective means of dramatizing the threat of circumstantial pressures and the adaptation that must follow. At the novel's centre is the motherless Molly Gibson, the daughter of the doctor of the small town of Hollingford, and the action of *Wives and Daughters* commences with her going to stay at Hamley Hall in order to act as a companion to Lady Hamley, a confirmed invalid. This visit also has the advantage of removing her from the attentions of one of her father's pupils, a circumstance which leads the widowed Dr Gibson to think that it would be advisable to remarry, and thus provide a suitable home atmosphere for his 17-year-old daughter. In choosing Clare – or Hyacinth, as she pretentiously prefers to be called – the former governess to the local aristocratic family, he lacks judgement. Gaskell provides a devastating critique of the new Mrs Gibson's snobbishness, pettiness, and selfishness: 'her superficial and flimsy character' (*WD* 144) – calculatingly double-edged, the narrative voice might have added, since Mrs Gibson voices sharp criticism when in private, yet speaks in company with 'that sweet, false tone' (*WD* 331) which goes through Molly like the scraping of a lead pencil on a slate.

Molly's own mother died before she could properly remember her, although the critical comments of her stepmother revive the memory of having her dark curls brushed by the maternal hand. She therefore does not approach Mrs Gibson with a direct point of comparison in mind (although the model of Lady Hamley, to whom she was, briefly, a substitute for the daughter she had lost, is tacitly there). Nonetheless, she experiences the awkwardness of calling her 'mamma' when, try as she might, there is little daughterly feeling in Molly towards Hyacinth. Far more troublesome is the fact that not only has Hyacinth disturbed the close bond of affection and understanding existing between Molly and her father, but Molly feels obliged to shelter from her father her own recognition that he must perceive and feel his new wife's failings. To disguise, to dissemble, even to avoid causing distress, is alien to Molly.

All virtuous nineteenth-century heroines, it might be said, find themselves in plots of others' making. Frequently, this entails little more than fitting in with the requirements of the romantic paradigm – in other words, the transmutation of daughters into wives – and in this instance Molly is no exception. No alternative future is postulated for either her or her stepsister Cynthia, other than that they should marry – and marry well. In the eyes of Cynthia's mother, this means marrying for money and status: thus she is keen to engineer her daughter's liaison with a Hamley heir: first with the older son, Osborne, and then, acting on overheard medical confidences which suggest that Osborne will not live long, she sets her matchmaking sights on Roger, the younger son. Captivated by Cynthia, who has a sexual and social self-awareness which Molly lacks, he needs little encouragement. Molly, discreetly and painfully in love with Roger herself, seems ostensibly on the outside of the matrimonial plotting, although Gaskell drops endless hints that she must ultimately be the preferred partner. We have no trouble in picking up the novelist's intentions from, for example, the fact that Molly is truly interested in the explorative naturalist's details in his letters home to Cynthia from his long overseas expedition, whilst her stepsister reads only the compliments addressed to her, and skips the rest. Molly's role is complicated, however, by the way in which she is trapped in far more testing plots than the waiting out of a happy conclusion. Whilst initially being kept in the dark about the domestic reason behind her being sent off to Hamley Hall, she subsequently finds herself in a succession of positions where she feels obliged to keep the secrets of others.

In particular, when reading in the library at Hamley Hall, Molly overhears Osborne in conversation with Roger, and mentioning his wife. This is, of course, hardly knowledge that she can reveal, which makes her extra uncomfortable through Hyacinth's matrimonial plotting. Only after Osborne's death is it incumbent upon Molly to reveal not just the widow's existence (and the fact that she is French, and had been a children's maid), but the existence of her son, the heir to the estate, to Squire Hamley. Keeping this knowledge to herself up to this point is a necessary, if alien and stressful act of concealment. Much more potentially damaging to Molly is the way in which Cynthia involves her in finally severing the links between herself and the insinuating land-agent Mr Preston, to whom the flirtatious girl had foolishly engaged herself a couple of years earlier. It is, of course, Molly who is seen to meet Mr Preston clandestinely, and suffers for it in Hollingford. Gossip, in *Wives and Daughters*, takes on a far more sinister and potentially damaging force than in *Cranford*. Rather than appearing in a positive light as a mode of women's narrative which acts as a counterpoint to the 'grand narratives' of public history, it functions as a form of verbal and social policing, ensuring that the actions of an individual are judged solely on unexamined pieces of external evidence. No longer, for that matter, are letters seen in an affirmative light, as providing alternative forms of female communication, but women are to be protected from their contents and their consequences (as Mr Gibson intercepts his pupil's love letter; as Molly receives Cynthia's letters back from Mr Preston). Letters have the power to disrupt, at least when the presence of men is significant to their writing or transmission.

Cynthia is forced to admit that she has, in fact if not in desire, been engaged to two men simultaneously. She writes to Roger to break off their engagement. Stung with a new idea, she looks Molly straight in the face, and says:

> 'Molly, Roger will marry you! See if it is not so! You two good –'
> But Molly pushed her away with a sudden violence of repulsion. 'Don't!' she said. She was crimson with shame and indignation. 'Your husband this morning! Mine to-night! What do you take him for?'
> 'A man!' smiled Cynthia. (*WD* 578–9)

Cynthia's pragmatism, born of experience, is set against Molly's idealism: it is also, of course, Cynthia's pragmatism and cheerful knowledge of the ways of the world that make her not just a foil for Cynthia, but an alternative focus of interest, perhaps, for a woman reader who is herself more mature than the naïve Molly. She exercises her 'unconscious power of fascination' as much on the reader as on Molly herself – thus placing us, of course, in the same category as the narrator puts Molly: among the 'susceptible' (WD 225). Cynthia wastes no time in finding a further fiancé, a London barrister, and marrying him. If, in Ruth, Gaskell was rather heavy-handed in her critical interrogation of the desirability of innocence, in Wives and Daughters she uses Molly, far more subtly, to raise a similar point. Molly's moral purity, a love of truthfulness associated with her dead mother, blinds her to any consideration of how others may view her, or project their motives onto her. Moreover, her naïvety, her unquestioning assumption of various values, are employed by Gaskell to call into question what have, up to the 1860s, been axiomatic values within her own writing.

This is particularly noticeable in relation to motherhood, and the discussion Molly has with Cynthia on the topic. Not all mothers, Wives and Daughters makes extremely clear, are good ones. Although the Hamley sons, in losing their mother, no longer have a 'kind, tender, mediatrix' (WD 319), Mrs Gibson's self-centredness has never allowed her to take on this role. Molly is shocked when Cynthia claims, after the girls have known each other only ten days, that she loves her better than she loves her mother. 'I don't think', Cynthia states bluntly, 'love for one's mother quite comes by nature; and remember how much I have been separated from mine!' (WD 228). This not only serves to remind the reader that even the most intimate human relationships may be ruled by reason as well as instinct; it raises the question as to whether feelings are innate, and perhaps thus connected with one's genealogy, or whether they are social in origin. This problem, closely bound in with the terms of evolutionary debate, is once again posed in connection with motherhood. Cynthia, hearing that Mr Preston is coming to live in Hollingford, conceives a desperate plan to go away as a governess: Molly tries to soothe her, 'taking Cynthia's passive hand, and stroking it softly – a mode of caressing that had come down to her from her mother – whether as an hereditary instinct, or as a lingering remembrance of the tender ways of the dead woman, Mr Gibson often wondered within himself when he observed it' (WD 344).

Wives and Daughters is unfinished. Gaskell died, suddenly,

before she could complete it. But it is clear that Roger and Molly will marry when he returns from his latest scientific expedition. This happy ending has conservative undertones: despite the fact that Molly readily absorbs scientific reading, considers a wasp's nest a desirable present, and is happy counting varieties of bees, it is never suggested that she might make a natural scientist too. Her talents render her, simply, a far more apt bride for Roger than Cynthia, with her dread of seriousness, could ever have been. Her suitability, too, comes from the fact that she is her father's daughter: Mr Gibson is a dedicated, perspicacious and self-consciously professional doctor, and the presence of the scientific at various levels in the projected marriage functions as a means of consolidating links between the professional classes and the landed gentry.

These are far from being the only links consolidated by the novel, however. Throughout her career, Elizabeth Gaskell recognized, as we have seen, the importance and effectiveness of accumulating telling detail. In *Wives and Daughters*, natural science not only provides a career for the male lead, but also constitutes an arena which can bring an individual respect and fame within London society, as well as being an interest, too, of the other men within this fictional society who maintain high moral standards: in particular, Mr Gibson and Lord Hollingford. Nineteenth-century fiction and natural science both demand a combination of the careful collection of empirical information and the noting of small variations and mutations, in order to monitor and, where possible, demonstrate how change occurs, slowly but inexorably, over time. Gaskell saw both the inevitability and the need for gradual change, whilst remaining apprehensive about the violence and destruction which revolutionary movements brought with them. In her fiction, she increasingly stands back as a commentator, and lets the facts of change, as well as more conservative counter-movements, speak for themselves.

8

Elizabeth Gaskell and Literary Criticism

Gaskell's interest in change, however, was not the aspect of her work which attracted earlier twentieth-century critics to her. Like so many mid-Victorian writers, she passed rapidly out of fashion. The prevailing attitude taken towards her in the first half of the twentieth century was typified by Lord David Cecil's now notorious characterization of Gaskell, in *Early Victorian Novelists*, as being 'all a woman was expected to be; gentle, domestic, tactful, unintellectual, prone to tears, easily shocked'. Her gender, and certain facts about her life – her family, her interest in domestic matters, her connections with Unitarianism – furnished a set of self-fulfilling prophecies when it came to locating certain properties in her writing. At the most extreme, even the care she puts into natural descriptions gets turned round so that her fiction could be described by Stanton Whitfield in 1929 as a 'nosegay of violets, honeysuckle, lavender, mignonette and sweet briar'. Although in some ways, as we have seen, *Cranford* may represent quite a bold experimentation in narrative techniques, it is not surprising, given the ostensibly quiet, private nature of its concerns, that this was the novel taken to typify her work at its best.

The 1950s, however, saw a dramatic realignment of Gaskell. No longer was she revered for her presumed femininity, but, following the publication of Kathleen Tillotson's *Novels of the Eighteen-Forties* in 1954, and the subsequent Marxist appropriation of her by Arnold Kettle (in the Pelican *From Dickens to Hardy* volume, 1958) and by Raymond Williams, in his highly influential *Culture and Society* (1958), Gaskell became, above all, known as a Social Problem novelist. Her treatment of the power relations of industrial societies meant that her works were initially read alongside such novels as Disraeli's *Sybil*, Kingsley's *Alton Locke*, and Dickens's *Hard Times*: in comparison with these writers, Williams singles her out for her 'combination of sympathetic observation and... a largely successful attempt at imaginative identification' – at least in the first part of *Mary Barton*, for he loses sympathy with the novel when, as he sees it, Gaskell falls prey to the temptation to melodrama, something which Williams reads as disrupting that unifying factor which animates the best writing, a powerful 'structure of feeling'. With criticism still dominated in the 1950s by the New Critical demand for unity in a work of art, even writing such as Williams's which is radical in many ways, fails to take account of the way in which ruptures and discontinuities within a text may not indicate an artistic lapse, but may themselves be symptomatic of competing ideological discourses circulating within a particular society. Williams's work was important, however, in establishing Gaskell's credentials as a 'serious' novelist, and her industrial works received by far the greatest amount of attention during the next couple of decades.

In recent years, however, particularly following the publication of Joseph Kestner's *Protest and Reform: The British Social Narrative by Women 1827–1867* (1985), she has been illuminatingly placed, not alongside her male contemporaries, but within a tradition of women who take on board public themes: writers like Frances Trollope, Harriet Martineau, Eliza Meteyard, and Charlotte Elizabeth Tonna. Simultaneously, those writers who continue to look at her within a more familiar canon of industrial writers, like Catherine Gallagher in *The Industrial Reformation of English Fiction* (1985) and Rosemarie Bodenheimer in *The Politics of Story in Victorian Social Fiction* (1988), have emphasized the power which Gaskell assigns to women. For Bodenheimer, *North and South* enacts the possibility of 'female paternalism', creating an image 'of woman's life as a negotiation of simultaneous crises, and a continual pressure of responsibility for actions that bear heavily on the lives of others'. The skills developed in running a family, in other words, may well be the skills which are most useful in managing industrial relations – although, as we saw earlier, the novel itself also makes it clear that it is dangerously misleading to collapse the models of children and workers. Gallagher is in many ways more subtle, focusing, as critics have increasingly come to do, not on the surface of Gaskell's writing, but on the more submerged ideological tendencies. She shows how the narrative of *North and South* questions the ethical connection that Margaret makes between private and public realms, and shows that although Margaret herself longs for a realm of absolute significance and unchanging values, meanings sanctioned by tradition and usage, these are meanings and associations which in fact must be dismantled in order that new bonds between individuals may be forged. Although Gallagher does not say so, the struggle that she locates in Margaret – between old and new value systems, between a nostalgic view of the past warmed by personal associations, and an acknowledgement of the necessity of change, with its concomitant new, fragile structures of understanding – is a tension which informs, as we have seen, a very great deal of Gaskell's writing.

Unsurprisingly, the biggest stimulus to rethinking Gaskell's works in recent decades has come from feminist criticism: not just that criticism which has encouraged the 'rediscovery' and re-evaluation of works by women and the traditions of which they have formed part, but that which looks for distinctive employment of language, of narrative strategies and of patterns of rhetoric which demonstrates how Gaskell, say, sought to empower women, and women's voices, in her writing. This criticism dates as far back, in fact, as Aina Rubenius's *The Woman Question in Mrs Gaskell's Life and Works*, published in 1950, but it received, like so much study of relatively undervalued nineteenth-century women writers, perhaps its greatest impetus from the appearance of Elaine Showalter's *A Literature of Their Own* in 1977. Although she writes relatively little directly about Gaskell, Showalter's contextualizing of the Victorian woman writer's self-consciousness about her dual role, as domestic and as professional figure, provided both materialist and psychological suggestions on which subsequent critics have built. The appeal of Gaskell to feminist critics has gone hand in hand with a broadening out of the Gaskell canon: not just have the more 'domestic' works, in particular *Cranford* and *Wives and Daughters*, been looked at afresh, but there has been a very noticeable growth of interest in her shorter fiction. It has been argued, for example by Carol Martin in an article called 'Gaskell's Ghosts: Truths in Disguise' (*Studies in the Novel*, 1989) that whilst in the realist novels each of the heroines is hemmed in by the demands of society that she acts in a 'womanly' fashion, Gaskell uses supernatural contexts to explore how a woman like Bridget Fitzgerald in 'The Old Nurse's Story' can be given an uncontrolled power to defy heaven and earth. This should not be understood as utopianism: lacking the differing kinds of support that society gives, such women may also be seen as victims, as outsiders, as we see in 'Lois the Witch'. Nonetheless, it is in some of the shorter pieces that Gaskell has been shown, simultaneously, both to challenge nineteenth-century trust in rationalism, and to undercut the social optimism which underpins her longer fictions.

Most influential and in many ways most impressive among feminist studies of Gaskell has been Patsy Stoneman's book in Harvester's Key Women Writers series. Stoneman connects class and gender in her study, showing that for women, 'politics begins with challenging the "private" acts which forbid them a public voice'. Perhaps in rather an essentialist manner, she believes that there is an 'authentic' woman's voice, which needs to find its expression without adopting masculinist language, rights, and principles: a need which is as strong now, Stoneman argues, as in Gaskell's time. Following the pioneering psychoanalytic work of Nancy Chodorow and Carol Gilligan, she locates this authenticity in woman's capacity for mothering and in the importance of the maternal bond: something which goes beyond strictly biological capacities to encompass woman's tendency to establish her identity, as she grows into adulthood, through bonding and identification with other women, rather than according to the Oedipal pattern of separation and differentiation from a paternal figure. Stoneman finds this bonding power of maternalism not just within the female characters of Gaskell's novels, but within some of the men's behaviour, as well – John Barton's care of his daughter, Mary, when she was left motherless; Benson's treatment of Ruth. Such bonding, such identification of interests, too, is, in Stoneman's reading of Gaskell, the principle which is most likely to bring classes together.

Perhaps the most illuminating recent studies of Gaskell have been those which have looked at her in a broader context of Victorian fiction, and indeed of culture and of narrative technique more generally. Robyn Warhol, in *Gendered Interventions, Narrative Discourse in the Victorian Novel* (1989) confronts something which is too frequently taken for granted in Gaskell criticism: the strong presence of an interventionist narrative commentary in the earlier fiction, and the fading of this voice in the later works. Initially, Warhol argues, these narrative interventions 'reveal an attempt to collapse the intra- and extra-diagetic, to bring together the worlds within and outside the fictions as though both existed on the same plane of reality': thus the 'I' may relatively comfortably be identified with the actual author, 'you' with the actual reader, setting up a 'bridge of sympathy which her strategies encourage the actual reader to cross in responding to the fiction and carrying that response over into extra-diagetic life'. Thus the narrator's disclaimers of access to complete knowledge of the events which she describes are on one level nonsense, a further form of fiction, but offer the air of being 'one fallible observer's account of actual events', and the appeals to our imaginative sympathy ask us to forget that we're reading a novel, as with the scene of John Barton's confession: 'Your heart would have ached to have seen the man, however hardly you might have judged his crime'. The inculcation of *personal* responsibility in her early readers was, argues Warhol, all-important to Gaskell. But after the publication of *Ruth*, observing the antagonistic, prudish reactions stirred up by this text, Gaskell's faith in her capacity to move her readers directly was shaken, Warhol maintains: hence, she stops intervening in her narratives, unconvinced of its effectiveness. Such a reading is certainly a corrective to the habitual version: that Gaskell became more assured and less clumsy in her command of narrative, and shows how she may in this matter, as in others, have been swayed by anxiety concerning response to her writing.

The theme of the professional novelist under pressure is central, too, to what is by far the most far-reaching and suggestive recent study of Gaskell, Hilary Schor's *Scheherezade in the Marketplace, Elizabeth Gaskell and the Victorian Novel* (1992). Schor starts from the assumption, hardly unique to her, that Gaskell sensed a tension between 'art' and 'duty', 'woman' and 'novelist', but goes on to develop her theme by saying that Gaskell's intense interest in publication and in acquiring a public voice, and her initial attempt, in *Mary Barton*, to write the fiction of those denied a voice within Victorian society 'led to an awareness of her own silencing, a sense of the ways that literary and cultural plots' – most conspicuously, within the conventions of Victorian fiction and society, the romance plot leading to marriage – 'shape our understanding of the world and limit our ability to describe it. Her experiments with literary form led her to examine the central stories of her culture, particularly the inscription of women as the (silent) other.' Partly, Schor is writing a materialist history, tracing Gaskell's complicated relationship with other writers, editors, publishers, and readers, showing how *their* expectations concerning dominant narratives had to be listened to and acceded to on occasion. She is particularly good on showing the manipulation Gaskell suffered at Dickens's hands once the publication of *North and South* was under way in *Household Words*. Dickens kept insisting that she hurry the plot along: Gaskell's position thus became that of one of the workers whose role she is in part describing, labouring in Dickens's literary factory according to his orders. This led, as she wrote to a friend, to her sense of the story being 'huddled & hurried up; especially in the rapidity with which the sudden death of Mr. Bell, succeeds to the sudden death of Mr. Hale. But what could I do? Every page was grudged me...' (*L* 328). Schor's point about Gaskell's interest in the varying ways in which we use systems of information to organize thought and judge behaviour comes out especially well when she writes of *Wives and Daughters*. The age's most characteristically male system of thought, she asserts – perhaps over-asserts – is the scientific thinking associated with Mr Gibson and with Roger:

> But if we take both biology and history as ways of organising what we see, of constructing narratives around facts, we are led to a parallel system in the novel: the female world of gossip, courtship narratives, and blackmail; the treacherous world of village women who create their own originating stories, and who deny, as fiercely as any of Darwin's bulldogs, the possibility of free movement and choice. Although the female world does not put itself forward as constructing reality in the way the Darwinian story does, it nonetheless shapes and explains behaviour, particularly the behaviour of women. In this novel, culture – in both its broadest and its narrowest sense, from biology to manners – becomes an imposing narrative.

What is impressive about Schor's work, what is symptomatic in it about the direction some of the most interesting criticism of Victorian literature is now taking, is its willingness to listen to and adopt the methodologies of other disciplines, in particular cultural anthropology and historiography. Both these disciplines have recently been concerned with the differing tools – linguistic, conceptual, narratological – which we tacitly employ in order to make sense of the world around us, in order to familiarize it, and give it some form of pattern, whether actual, wished-for, or delusory. Despite its own particular conventions, the making of realist fictions is analogous to the process of understanding culture in which each of us is involved on a daily basis.

Yet just recently, however, some critical attention seems to have swung back to Gaskell the woman. The oddest manifestation of this is Felicia Bonaparte's study *The Gypsy-Bachelor of Manchester: The Life of Mrs Gaskell's Demon* (1992). She argues that 'Mrs Gaskell' was a constructed identity behind which the 'real' Elizabeth Gaskell, consciously or unconsciously, hid. Just as she wrote in *Sylvia's Lovers* 'No one knew much of what was passing in Sylvia; she did not know herself', so, Bonaparte asserts, Gaskell had a powerful inner life in continual conflict with the 'respectable' choices which she made not only in her own life, but around which she structured her plots. This rebellion against orthodoxy, Bonaparte maintains, does not rise to the surface in isolated disruptive moments, but persists as a subtext to her entire oeuvre. By contrast, Jenny Uglow's superbly researched, authoritative biography of Elizabeth Gaskell (1993) gives one a great deal of material through which to contextualize Gaskell's writings, and provides just enough literary analysis to demonstrate how both private fears and concerns, and publically debated issues, continually find their way into Gaskell's fiction, biography, and other writings. There is no attempt to presume that she has some privileged, empathic route into the secret heart of her writer, as in Bonaparte's extraordinary attempt to bring the *textual* unconscious to the fore and pass off its strains and contradictions as the rebellious, iconoclastic self of the author.

And yet, one thing that Bonaparte's book does make one think about is what, in Gaskell's writing, constitutes the 'self'? By this, I do not mean the author's self, but the concept of 'selfhood' as understood, or dimly perceived, both by characters themselves and by the narrators. When one considers the directions which criticism of Gaskell may take in the future, this whole question of the construction of selfhood – within what social anthropologists might call a circumscribed *habitus*, or environment where cultural values are legibly encoded; or in relation to the delineation, both explicitly and silently, of an individual's unconscious – is something that profitably may be examined further. So, too, despite the considerable amount of attention which Gaskell's fiction has received from feminist critics, is the question of gender – in particular the interrogative depiction of *masculinity* in the novels. What challenges was Gaskell laying down through her treatment of *men*? And another line of enquiry which has not received its full due is the connections between Gaskell and aesthetics: how does she frame her scenes? what kind of perspectives does she employ? how does she use the vocabulary of space, of colour, of line? how does she manipulate fictional, and, by implication, visual conventions when it comes to depicting landscapes, or the appearance of the city? And where does one locate *her* aesthetics in the midst of the shifts that were taking place in Victorian taste with the growth in consumerism and markets for aesthetic objects? Once again, we find ourselves considering Gaskell's relationship to a changing world.

Society, as Elizabeth Gaskell carefully observed it, expressed itself through a number of competing discourses: discourses both in the theoretical sense of systems and languages of classification and explanation, and in the more everyday sense of conversation. Gaskell certainly used the conventions of her day, particularly the romance plot, in order to structure her fictions. However, her fictions also demonstrate the dangers, and restrictions, of being trapped within social conventions and ways of thinking. Whether she is dealing with the theme of the seduced young girl or the lack of comprehension that frequently exists between different classes; whether she is satirizing Francophobia or the importance of wearing the right kind of bonnet, Gaskell shows that rigid conventions are damaging to the important goal of human understanding and sympathy. She sees her role, as expressed through fiction, to be that of the 'kind, tender, mediatrix' (*WD* 319). Her novels and shorter stories are concerned with the breaking down of barriers: between individuals, between classes, between genders, between intellectual disciplines. Simultaneously, however, her fiction derives much of its power from her dramatization of the tension created by the barriers themselves.

In her analysis of her own character, Elizabeth Gaskell wrote of the impossibility of reconciling the warring parts. However much she might hanker after the notion of a unified self, she accepts that it is an unachievable ideal. Similarly, the plots of her fiction show a strong drive towards resolution, towards the achievement of authoritative positions: yet they always leave the reader with unanswered, perhaps unanswerable questions about the nature of desire, of power, of the direction in which society will develop. The strength of Gaskell's fiction lies in her capacity to dramatize, investigate, and exploit the forces of social change, the effects of which continued to resonate long after her death.

Select Bibliography

WORKS BY ELIZABETH GASKELL

All of Gaskell's major works and almost all her short stories are available in Penguin and World's Classics paperbacks. The titles and dates of first publication are included in the Biographical Outline on p. ix.

BIOGRAPHICAL AND CRITICAL STUDIES

Auerbach, Nina, *Communities of Women: An Idea in Fiction* (Harvard University Press, 1978). Chapter 3 (pp. 77–97) places the society of *Cranford*, with its 'self-protective whimsy', alongside other nineteenth-century depictions of female communities, from Jane Austen to Gissing.

Bodenheimer, Rosemarie, *The Politics of Story in Victorian Social Fiction* (Cornell University Press, 1988). In chapter 1 (pp. 53–68) Bodenheimer treats the politics of negotiation in *North and South* within the context of other fictional portrayals of female paternalists; chapter 3 (pp. 150–65) discusses the maternal resonances of the use of pastoral in *Ruth*.

Craik, W. A., *Elizabeth Gaskell and the English Provincial Novel* (Methuen, 1975). A highly conservative discussion of Gaskell, reading her in the light of other novelists (Trollope, George Eliot, Hardy) who treat non-urban environments.

David, Deirdre, *Fictions of Resolution in Three Victorian Novels: 'North and South', 'Our Mutual Friend' and 'Daniel Deronda'* (Macmillan, 1981). Considers the problems of reaching satisfactory points of closure in Victorian fiction.

Dolin, Tim, '*Cranford* and the Victorian Collection', *Victorian Studies*, 36 (1993), 179–206.

Eagleton, Terry, '*Sylvia's Lovers* and Legality', *Essays in Criticism*, 26 (1977), 17–27.

Easson, Angus, *Elizabeth Gaskell* (Routledge and Kegan Paul, 1979).

Usefully puts Gaskell in a full social context.

Gallagher, Catherine, *The Industrial Reformation of English Fiction: Social Discourse and Narrative Form 1832–1867* (University of Chicago Press, 1985). Sophisticated and stimulating readings of *Mary Barton* (pp. 62–87), stressing the novel's generic eclecticism, and of *North and South* (pp. 166–84), examining the contradictions inherent in the ideologies of public and private spheres which Gaskell uses.

Gérin, Winifred, *Elizabeth Gaskell* (Oxford University Press, 1976). Supplanted by Jenny Uglow's biography, but nonetheless contains useful material.

Gillooly, Eileen, 'Humor as Daughterly Defense in *Cranford*', *ELH*, 59 (1992), 883–910.

Harman, Barbara Leah, 'In Promiscuous Company: Female Public Appearance in Elizabeth Gaskell's *North and South*', *Victorian Studies*, 31 (1988) 351–74. Shows how women's appearances in public readily took on a pejorative significance during the Victorian period.

Homans, Margaret, *Bearing the Word: Language and Female Experience in Nineteenth-Century Women's Writing* (University of Chicago Press, 1986). Chapters 9 and 10 (pp. 223–76) illuminatingly examine the treatment of motherhood and of maternal imagery in Gaskell's writing.

Jordan, Elaine, 'Spectres and Scorpions: Allusion and Confusion in *Mary Barton*', *Literature and History* 7 (1981), 48–61.

Kestner, Joseph, *Protest and Reform: The British Social Narrative by Women 1827–1867* (University of Wisconsin Press, 1985). Interestingly situates Gaskell's fiction among the range of 'social problem' fictions by women far less well remembered today.

Lansbury, Coral, *Elizabeth Gaskell: The Novel of Social Class* (Elek, 1975). Enthusiastic, if sometimes slightly overstated analysis.

Lucas, John, 'Mrs Gaskell and Brotherhood', in David Howard, John Lucas and John Goode (eds.) *Tradition and Tolerance in Nineteenth Century Fiction* (Routledge and Kegan Paul, 1966), pp. 141–205. Informative and detailed on Gaskell's knowledge and treatment of the working classes, discussing her industrial fiction alongside other 'social problem' novels.

Nestor, Pauline, *Female Friendships and Communities: Charlotte Brontë, George Eliot, Elizabeth Gaskell* (Oxford University Press, 1985). Good on Gaskell's relations with other women writers, and her concern with the problems of women's occupations.

Schor, Hilary M., *Scheherezade in the Marketplace: Elizabeth Gaskell and the Victorian Novel* (Oxford University Press, 1992). Illuminating: places Gaskell's writing in the context of the problems facing a Victorian woman writer in establishing an authoritative voice, and looks at the material and social implications of her modes of publication.

Stoneman, Patsy, *Elizabeth Gaskell* (Harvester, 1987). A thoughtful, informed and stimulating feminist approach to Gaskell's life and fiction.

Uglow, Jenny, *Elizabeth Gaskell: A Habit of Stories* (Faber and Faber, 1993) is the authoritative study of Gaskell's life. Knowledgeable, thorough in its research and thoughtful in its analysis, this is an exemplary biography.

Warhol, Robyn R., *Gendered Interventions: Narrative Discourse in the Victorian Novel* (Rutgers University Press, 1989). Analyses the way in which the first-person 'omniscient' narrator gradually becomes less prominent in Gaskell's fiction, and sets her use of the narrative voice alongside that of contemporary novelists.

Webb, R.K., 'The Gaskells as Unitarians', in Joanne Shattock (ed.), *Dickens and Other Victorians: Essays in Honour of Philip Collins* (Macmillan, 1988). Important religious contextualization.

Williams, Raymond, *Culture and Society, 1780–1950* (Chatto and Windus, 1958). Chapter 5, 'The Industrial Novels', offers a pioneering treatment of Gaskell as a writer of 'social problem' fiction.

Index

Recent and Forthcoming Titles in the New Series of

WRITERS AND THEIR WORK

WRITERS AND THEIR WORK

RECENT & FORTHCOMING TITLES

Title	Author
Aphra Behn	*Sue Wiseman*
Angela Carter	*Lorna Sage*
Children's Literature	*Kimberley Reynolds*
John Clare	*John Lucas*
Joseph Conrad	*Cedric Watts*
John Donne	*Stevie Davies*
Henry Fielding	*Jenny Uglow*
Elizabeth Gaskell	*Kate Flint*
William Golding	*Kevin McCarron*
Hamlet	*Ann Thompson & Neil Taylor*
David Hare	*Jeremy Ridgman*
Tony Harrison	*Joe Kelleher*
William Hazlitt	*J.B. Priestley; R.L. Brett (introduction by Michael Foot)*
George Herbert	*T.S. Eliot (introduction by Peter Porter)*
Henry James - The Later Writing	*Barbara Hardy*
King Lear	*Terence Hawkes*
Doris Lessing	*Elizabeth Maslen*
David Lodge	*Bernard Bergonzi*
Christopher Marlowe	*Thomas Healy*
Andrew Marvell	*Annabel Patterson*
Ian McEwan	*Kiernan Ryan*
Walter Pater	*Laurel Brake*
Jean Rhys	*Helen Carr*
Dorothy Richardson	*Carol Watts*
The Sensation Novel	*Lyn Pykett*
Edmund Spenser	*Colin Burrow*
Leo Tolstoy	*John Bayley*
Charlotte Yonge	*Alethea Hayter*

TITLES IN PREPARATION

Title	Author
Peter Ackroyd	*Susana Onega*
Antony and Cleopatra	*Ken Parker*
W.H. Auden	*Stan Smith*
Jane Austen	*Robert Clark*
Elizabeth Bowen	*Maud Ellmann*
Emily Brontë	*Stevie Davies*
A.S. Byatt	*Richard Todd*
Lord Byron	*J. Drummond Bone*
Geoffrey Chaucer	*Steve Ellis*
Caryl Churchill	*Elaine Aston*
S.T. Coleridge	*Stephen Bygrave*
Charles Dickens	*Rod Mengham*

TITLES IN PREPARATION

Title	Author
George Eliot	*Josephine McDonagh*
E.M. Forster	*Nicholas Royle*
Brian Friel	*Geraldine Higgins*
Graham Greene	*Peter Mudford*
Thomas Hardy	*Peter Widdowson*
Seamus Heaney	*Andrew Murphy*
Henry IV	*Peter Bogdanov*
Henrik Ibsen	*Sally Ledger*
James Joyce	*Steven Connor*
Rudyard Kipling	*Jan Montefiore*
Franz Kafka	*Michael Wood*
John Keats	*Kelvin Everest*
Philip Larkin	*Laurence Lerner*
D.H. Lawrence	*Linda Ruth Williams*
A Midsummer Night's Dream	*Helen Hackett*
William Morris	*Anne Janowitz*
Brian Patten	*Linda Cookson*
Alexander Pope	*Pat Rogers*
Sylvia Plath	*Elizabeth Bronfen*
Richard II	*Margaret Healy*
Lord Rochester	*Peter Porter*
Romeo and Juliet	*Sasha Roberts*
Christina Rossetti	*Katherine Burlinson*
Salman Rushdie	*Damian Grant*
Stevie Smith	*Alison Light*
Sir Walter Scott	*John Sutherland*
Wole Soyinka	*Mpalive Msiska*
Jonathan Swift	*Claude Rawson*
The Tempest	*Gordon McMullan*
J.R.R. Tolkien	*Charles Moseley*
Mary Wollstonecraft	*Jane Moore*
Evelyn Waugh	*Malcolm Bradbury*
Angus Wilson	*Peter Conradi*
Virginia Woolf	*Laura Marcus*
William Wordsworth	*Nicholas Roe*
Working Class Fiction	*Ian Haywood*
W.B. Yeats	*Ed Larrissy*

RECENT &
FORTHCOMING TITLES

DORIS LESSING
Elizabeth Maslen

Covering a wide range of Doris Lessing's works up to 1992, including all her novels and a selection of her short stories and non-fictional writing, this study demonstrates how Lessing's commitment to political and cultural issues and her explorations of inner space have remained unchanged throughout her career. Maslen also examines Lessing's writings in the context of the work of Bakhtin and Foucault, and of feminist theories.

Elizabeth Maslen is Senior Lecturer in English at Queen Mary and Westfield College, University of London.

0 7463 0705 5 paperback 80pp

JOSEPH CONRAD
Cedric Watts

This authoritative introduction to the range of Conrad's work draws out the distinctive thematic preoccupations and technical devices running through the main phases of the novelist's literary career. Watts explores Conrad's importance and influence as a moral, social and political commentator on his times and addresses recent controversial developments in the evaluation of this magisterial, vivid, complex and problematic author.

"...balanced insights into the controversies surrounding Conrad".
Times Educational Supplement.

Cedric Watts, Professor of English at the University of Sussex, is recognized internationally as a leading authority on the life and works of Joseph Conrad.

0 7463 0737 3 paperback 80pp

JOHN DONNE
Stevie Davies

Raising a feminist challenge to the body of male criticism which congratulates Donne on the 'virility' of his writing, Dr Davies' stimulating and accessible introduction to the full range of the poet's work sets it in the wider cultural, religious and political context conditioning the mind of this turbulent and brilliant poet. Davies also explores the profound emotionalism of Donne's verse and offers close, sensitive readings of individual poems.

Stevie Davies is a literary critic and novelist who has written on a wide range of literature.

0 7463 0738 1 paperback 96pp

THE SENSATION NOVEL
Lyn Pykett

A 'great fact' in the literature of its day, a 'disagreeable' sign of the times, or an ephemeral minor sub-genre? What was the sensation novel, and why did it briefly dominate the literary scene in the 1860s? This wide-ranging study analyses the broader significance of the sensation novel as well as looking at it in its specific cultural context.

Lyn Pykett is Senior Lecturer in English at the University of Wales in Aberystwyth.

0 7463 0725 X paperback 96pp

CHRISTOPHER MARLOWE
Thomas Healy

The first study for many years to explore the whole range of Marlowe's writing, this book uses recent ideas about the relation between literature and history, popular and élite culture, and the nature of Elizabethan theatre to reassess his significance. An ideal introduction to one of the most exciting and innovative of English writers, Thomas Healy's book provides fresh insights into all of Marlowe's important works.

Thomas Healy is Senior Lecturer in English at Birkbeck College, University of London.

0 7463 0707 1 paperback 96pp

ANDREW MARVELL
Annabel Patterson

This state-of-the art guide to one of the seventeenth century's most intriguing poets examines Marvell's complex personality and beliefs and provides a compelling new perspective on his work. Annabel Patterson – one of the leading Marvell scholars – provides comprehensive introductions to Marvell's different self-representations and places his most famous poems in their original context.

Annabel Patterson is Professor of English at Yale University and author of *Marvell and the Civic Crown* (1978).

0 7463 0715 2 paperback 96pp

JOHN CLARE
John Lucas

Setting out to recover Clare – whose work was demeaned and damaged by the forces of the literary establishment – as a great poet, John Lucas offers the reader the chance to see the life and work of John Clare, the 'peasant poet' from a new angle. His unique and detailed study portrays a knowing, articulate and radical poet and thinker writing as much out of a tradition of song as of poetry. This is a comprehensive and detailed account of the man and the artist which conveys a strong sense of the writer's social and historical context.

*"Clare's unique greatness is asserted and proved in John Lucas's brilliant, sometimes moving, discourse." **Times Educational Supplement.***

John Lucas has written many books on nineteenth- and twentieth-century literature, and is himself a talented poet. He is Professor of English at Loughborough University.

0 7463 0729 2 paperback 96pp

GEORGE HERBERT
T.S. Eliot
With a new introductory essay by **Peter Porter**

Another valuable reissue from the original series, this important study – one of T. S. Eliot's last critical works – examines the writings of George Herbert, considered by Eliot to be one of the loveliest and most profound of English poets. The new essay by well-known poet and critic Peter Porter reassesses Eliot's study, as well as providing a new perspective on Herbert's work. Together, these critical analyses make an invaluable contribution to the available literature on this major English poet.

0 7463 0746 2 paperback 80pp £5.99

CHILDREN'S LITERATURE
Kimberley Reynolds

Children's literature has changed dramatically in the last hundred years and this book identifies and analyses the dominant genres which have evolved during this period. Drawing on a wide range of critical and cultural theories, Kimberley Reynolds looks at children's private reading, examines the relationship between the child reader and the adult writer, and draws some interesting conclusions about children's literature as a forum for shaping the next generation and as a safe place for developing writers' private fantasies.

*"The book manages to cover a surprising amount of ground . . . without ever seeming perfunctory. It is a very useful book in an area where a short pithy introduction like this is badly needed." **Times Educational Supplement***

Kimberley Reynolds lectures in English and Women's Studies at Roehampton Institute, where she also runs the Children's Literature Research Unit.

0 7463 0728 4 paperback 112pp

WILLIAM GOLDING
Kevin McCarron

This comprehensive study takes an interdisciplinary approach to the work of William Golding, placing particular emphasis on the anthropological perspective missing from most other texts on his writings. The book covers all his novels, questioning the status of *Lord of the Flies* as his most important work, and giving particular prominence to *The Inheritors, Pincher Martin, The Spire* and The Sea Trilogy. This in-depth evaluation provides many new insights into the works of one of the twentieth century's greatest writers.

Kevin McCarron is Lecturer in English at Roehampton Institute, where he teaches Modern English and American Literature. He has written widely on the work of William Golding.

0 7463 0735 7 paperback 80pp

WALTER PATER
Laurel Brake

This is the only critical study devoted to the works of Pater, an active participant in the nineteenth-century literary marketplace as an academic, journalist, critic, writer of short stories and novelist. Approaching Pater's writings from the perspective of cultural history, this book covers all his key works, both fiction and non-fiction.

"...grounded in an unmatched scholarly command of Pater's life and writing."
English Association Newsletter

Laurel Brake is Lecturer in Literature at Birkbeck College, University of London, and has written widely on Victorian literature and in particular on Pater.

0 7463 0716 0 paperback 96pp

ANGELA CARTER
Lorna Sage

Angela Carter was probable the most inventive British novelist of her generation. In this fascinating study, Lorna Sage argues that one of the reasons for Carter's enormous success is the extraordinary intelligence with which she read the cultural signs of our times – from structuralism and the study of folk tales in the 1960s – to, more recently, fairy stories and gender politics. The book explores the roots of Carter's originality and covers all her novels, as well as some short stories and non-fiction.

"...this reappraisal of an interesting novelist explores the roots of her originality .. . a useful introduction to the work of Angela Carter.' **Sunday Telegraph**

Lorna Sage teaches at the University of East Anglia, where she is currently Dean of the School of English and American Studies.

0 7463 0727 6 paperback 96pp

IAN McEWAN
Kiernan Ryan

This is the first book-length study of one of the most original and exciting writers to have emerged in Britain in recent years. It provides an introduction to the whole range of McEwan's work, examining his novels, short stories and screenplays in depth and tracing his development from the 'succès de scandale' of *First Love, Last Rites* to the haunting vision of the acclaimed *Black Dogs*.

"(Written with)...conviction and elegance." **The Irish Times**

Kiernan Ryan is Fellow and Director of Studies in English at New Hall, University of Cambridge.

0 7463 0742 X paperback 80pp

ELIZABETH GASKELL
Kate Flint

Recent critical appraisal has focused on Gaskell both as a novelist of industrial England and on her awareness of the position of women and the problems of the woman writer. Kate Flint reveals how for Gaskell the condition of women was inseparable from broader issues of social change. She shows how recent modes of feminist criticism and theories of narrative work together to illuminate the radicalism and experimentalism which we find in Gaskell's fiction.

Kate Flint is University Lecturer in Victorian and Modern English Literature, and Fellow of Linacre College, Oxford.

0 7463 0718 7 paperback 96pp

KING LEAR
Terence Hawkes

In his concise but thorough analysis of *King Lear* Terence Hawkes offers a full and clear exposition of its complex narrative and thematic structure. By examining the play's central preoccupations and through close analysis of the texture of its verse he seeks to locate it firmly in its own history and the social context to which, clearly, it aims to speak. The result is a challenging critical work which both deepens understanding of this great play and illuminates recent approaches to it.

Terence Hawkes has written several books on both Shakespeare and modern critical theory. He is Professor of English at the University of Wales, Cardiff.

0 7463 0739 X paperback 96pp

JEAN RHYS
Helen Carr

Drawing on her own experience of alienation and conflict as a white-Creole woman, Rhys's novels are recognised as important explorations of gender and colonial power relations. Using feminist and post-colonial theory, Helen Carr's study places Rhys's work in relation to modernist and postmodernist writing and looks closely at how autobiographical material is used by the writer to construct a devastating critique of the greed and cruelty of patriarchy and the Empire.

Helen Carr is Lecturer in English at Goldsmiths College, University of London.

0 7463 0717 9 paperback 96pp

DOROTHY RICHARDSON
Carol Watts

Dorothy Richardson is a major modern novelist whose work is only now beginning to attract the attention of critics, feminists, and cultural theorists. She was one of the earliest novelists to consider the importance of developing a new aesthetic form to represent women's experience and in doing so, she explored many of the new art forms of the twentieth century. Carol Watt's book is an innovative study of her extraordinary thirteen-volume novel, *Pilgrimage* and offers an exciting challenge to the common readings of literary modernism.

Carol Watts is Lecturer in English Literature at Birkbeck College, University of London.

0 7463 0708 X paperback 112pp

APHRA BEHN
Sue Wiseman

Aphra Behn was prolific in all the most commercial genres of her time and wrote widely on many of the most controversial issues of her day – sexual and cultural difference, slavery, politics, and money. Bringing together an analysis of the full range of her writing in poetry, prose and drama, this is the first book-length critical study of Aphra Behn's work, much of which has been hitherto relatively neglected.

Sue Wiseman is Lecturer in English at the University of Warwick.

0 7463 0709 8 paperback 96pp

DAVID HARE
Jeremy Ridgman

David Hare is one of the most prolific, challenging, and culturally acclaimed playwrights in Britain today. Jeremy Ridgman's study focuses on the dramatic method that drives the complex moral and political narratives of Hare's work. He considers its relationship to its staging and performance, looking in particular at the dramatist's collaborations with director, designer, and performer. Hare's writing for the theatre since 1970 is set alongside his work for television and film and his achievements as director and translator, to provide a detailed insight into key areas of his dramatic technique particularly dialogue, narrative, and epic form.

Jeremy Ridgman is Senior Lecturer in the Department of Drama and Theatre Studies at Roehampton Institute, London

0 7463 0774 8 paperback 96pp

TONY HARRISON
Joe Kelleher

Tony Harrison has been acclaimed worldwide, not only for his slim volumes of poetry but also for his lyric sequences and long poems, for his adaptations and original plays for the theatre, his opera libretti, and his verse films for television. Kelleher argues that Harrison's unique achievement is to ransack a whole range of traditions in order to carve out in verse, a very innovative and contemporary mode of public utterance.

Joe Kelleher is a playwright and Lecturer in Drama at Roehampton Institute.

0 7463 0789 6 paperback 96pp

CHARLOTTE YONGE
Alethea Hayter

Charlotte Yonge was a best-selling Victorian author and widely admired by her greatest literary contemporaries in the mid-ninteenth century but for the next hundred years, ignored or vilified by critics. Her work has only recently begun to receive the
historians and feminists. Alethea H
surveys the full range of her work
and wild-life, as well as her family
children's books. Yonge emerges a
the renewed interest in her and he

Alethea Hayter is a literary critic a
number of books on nineteenth-ce

0 7463 0781 0 paperback 96pp